SILENT FRANK COCHRANE

To look at history largely through the eyes and movements of the actors who occupy the stage at front and centre . . . is appropriate, but there may also be new perspectives and evaluations if we put ourselves in the position of those who were at sidestage, or in the wings . . .

We must have the lives of the great men; we can also profit from the recreation of the lives of those who were less the pilots than the symbols of their times. . . . In their usually undramatic way, they were as much the Makers of Canada as the classic heroes.

Alan Wilson,
The Canadian Historical Association,
Report, 1965

SILENT FRANK COCHRANE

The North's First Great Politician

Scott Young & Astrid Young

MACMILLAN OF CANADA
TORONTO

ISBN 0-7705-0889-8

Printed in Canada by
The Hunter Rose Company
for The Macmillan Company of Canada Limited
70 Bond Street, Toronto 2

SILENT FRANK COCHRANE

CHAPTER ONE

The man the people and politicians of his time called Silent
Frank Cochrane died in 1919 after an extraordinary political
career. Without any more experience in politics than could be
obtained by two terms as a councillor in Sudbury (where he
was a successful hardware merchant), three terms as mayor
there, and an unsuccessful try in 1902 for the West Nipissing
seat in the Ontario legislature, he was handed major cabinet
posts immediately after Conservative upsets in Ontario (1905)
and in the Canadian general election of 1911. This although
he had not run for office in either of those elections.

When Premier James Pliny Whitney took Cochrane into
his Ontario cabinet in 1905, a member who had just been
elected (in the same general area where Cochrane had been
beaten in 1902) resigned to make way. There was no subsequent by-election. In a rare show of unanimity (or, some
charged, collusion) both Liberals and Conservatives nominated Cochrane, and he took the seat by acclamation.

Six years later when Sir Robert Borden became Canadian
prime minister by defeating Sir Wilfrid Laurier in the reciprocity election of 1911, one of his first acts was to induce Frank
Cochrane, his Ontario organizer, to resign from the Ontario

cabinet and join the federal cabinet's front rank. Again a seat was opened to make this possible by acclamation.

Overwhelming or crystal-clear reasons for this tendency in government leaders of that time to beat a path to Silent Frank Cochrane's door are not easy to come by. He was as sparing in saving personal papers and correspondence as he was in speech. He did not encourage lengthy newspaper interviews, and in the House his answers even to quite long and involved questions were often a simple yes or no. "Cochrane has the clam beaten to a finish for habitual reticence," one Ontario legislature reporter wrote early in Silent Frank's career. Another gave the opinion: "Cochrane would rather be kicked than make a speech." The Rt. Hon. Arthur Meighen, like Cochrane a member of the powerful inner core of the Borden cabinet, once wrote: "As a parliamentarian he was the most silent man I have ever known occupying a position in the ministry. On one occasion I recall a virulent attack of great length that had been made upon him and his administration. Everyone was waiting anxiously for his reply. As nearly as I can remember this is what he said: 'Mr. Speaker, I have heard this long attack. There is absolutely nothing to it.' Then he sat down. What he said was true—no repetition of the subject of that attack ever was made."

A man who meted out his words so frugally might have been expected to be handicapped in politics; but this was not the case with Cochrane. He only lost one election in his life, winning his last one in 1917, even while too ill to campaign much. He occupied a position of firm influence during one six-year era of Ontario politics beginning in 1905 when the Conservatives laid such a firm base that the Liberals (who had dominated the province for three decades earlier) have been able to win only one election since. And he was counted one of the strongest movers in the federal government from 1911 on, when Canada took giant steps on the way to full nationhood.

What motivated him? What was his aim? It would help if

Silent Frank Cochrane had left somewhere a line or two on what he sought in life. But his personal and official papers no longer exist, destroyed either at his own direction (which would have been in character) or, after his death, without it. His original entry into politics seemed to be because he was devoted to the North and felt it was neglected by governments. Once he confided to his son Wilbur that "the brains in Ontario end at Barrie." He clearly meant that they were all north of that town, leaving Toronto brainless. Apart from that, he seemed to like politics for itself.

Remarkably little is known about his early years, before he turned up as an imposingly big (six feet, three inches; 200 pounds) hardware clerk in the northern Ontario town of Mattawa in the early 1880s. Even newspaper and magazine articles written when he was still around to answer specific questions tend to skim over his first thirty years. One writer told of Cochrane's spending two days in a tree with a pack of timber wolves snapping around the base—but he didn't tell when it happened, where, under what circumstances, or even how he escaped.

Sir Herbert Holt, when he was president of the Canadian Pacific Railway, once told Wilbur Cochrane, Silent Frank's son, that during the building of the C.P.R. he'd met Frank Cochrane and "he could clean out a drunken sleeping car quicker than anyone I've ever seen in my life." The inference being, with his fists if necessary. Once again, the exact circumstances are lost.

Wilbur Cochrane was able to sketch in the thirty years after his father's birth on November 18, 1852, in Clarenceville, Quebec, only to the extent that he had gone to Chicago and worked at the predecessor of the present Marshall Field store, until fired for knocking down his superior in a fight. From Chicago he proceeded to the roistering Ottawa River town of Pembroke, Ontario, in the late 1870s, to work in a hardware store owned by a great-uncle named Hunter. He quit there to work for a competitor, Dunlap and Chapman. In 1882 he married Dunlap's daughter, Alice, and was sent 91 miles on along the railroad line to manage a new branch of the Dunlap and Chapman store, in Mattawa. Most hardware business in those days was with the railroad, or with the large timber companies logging the areas through which railroads passed. In the next few years there was not enough business to occupy Cochrane full time. He worked in the woods for a while— including his winter encounter with the timber wolves. But then as the hardware business prospered his name began to turn up from time to time in local news reports on town affairs. In Mattawa he had rented a house next door to his store. The house had an outdoor privy, a well in the yard, a big cookstove in the kitchen—a place indistinguishable from many of its neighbours in a frontier community where no building was more than two storeys high and the better ones were fronted by board sidewalks; all the streets were mud.

The only hint that he was already becoming involved in politics in Mattawa is a memory of his son's, that in 1890 Sir John A. Macdonald became ill on a train passing through. There was no hospital in Mattawa, so John A. spent the next few days on a sofa in the Cochrane parlour in their rented house. Cochrane must have been the principal Conservative in the town at that time; or, at the very least, the principal Conservative who also had a spare bed. The house is still standing in Mattawa, now being used as a barber shop. Wilbur Cochrane, then six years old, used to go down the street twice a day at John A.'s bidding, to pick up a bottle of whisky from McGoogan's store and bring it back to the great man.

Later that year, Cochrane went into business for himself. He bought out a merchant named D. R. McPhail, 121 miles farther west, at Sudbury. This was the pattern of frontier business in those days—following the railroad to where there were virgin timber limits to be cut, or new mineral discoveries to be developed. The new business was chancy enough that at first he didn't have the money to bring his wife and three children (Wilbur, 6; Edith, 2; and Ogden, an infant) with him. But in a few months on one of his visits home he began to plan the move with his wife. He took his family to Sudbury in 1891, again to a rented house. This one was on a grander scale than the one at Mattawa, with seven bedrooms. There were three horses (a team for store deliveries, and another used as a driver—that day's equivalent of the family car). There was also a cow to supply milk for the household, which by then included two hired girls who did the housework and were paid $7 a month each.

Sudbury, a village of a few hundred people, already seemed on the decline to some people by the time Cochrane arrived. The pattern had been established elsewhere. As the railroad builders moved steadily west in the early 1880s, such settlements as Mattawa, North Bay, and Sturgeon Falls flared briefly into prominence and then abruptly declined as work moved westward. When steel reached Sudbury in 1883, the population soared from nothing to about 1,500. But within a few years it had dropped to 300 permanent residents, most of them surviving one way or another from working timber limits that had been too far from any river to be useful before the railroad came and provided an alternative route to market. The timber wouldn't last long, everyone knew. But Sudbury had been given a second chance. Cutting the railroad right-of-way, work crews had happened upon mineral-bearing rock. The activities of booming prospectors revived local business.

By 1890 when Cochrane arrived there was still no certainty that the mines would provide a stable economy, but the chance was there. Cochrane, while he had made some money from timber, was quoted in one of his few surviving remarks of that time as saying that what was below the ground was a lot more valuable than what was above it. And to get the minerals out required hardware. He sold it.

Sudbury in 1893 had grown again to 1,000 population and was incorporated as a town. But, as noted by D. M. Le-Bourdais in his book *Sudbury Basin*, "it was yet without sidewalks, and sewage ran in the gutters. Most of the citizens got their water from a spring that bubbled out of a gravel pit, and householders paid a water peddler to keep their barrels filled."

In 1893 Frank Cochrane first began to be mentioned in the *Sudbury Journal*, a weekly that also carried his hardware advertisements. By then he seems to have been on the course that would make him, in the long run, a nationally known politician. He helped solicit prizes for exhibitions, appeared before the town council to challenge the whole system of assessment in the community, was on the executive of the first local Liberal-Conservative association, as the Tory party was called in those days. He spoke at public meetings on such problems as which community should became the county town for the new judicial district of Nipissing (he thought a referendum of voters should decide). He was treasurer of the Agricultural Society, and he and his wife were patrons of the Sudbury Rifle Association.

Such events may seem picayune but indicate that he was working his way up on two fronts that contributed strongly to his subsequent power in Ontario politics: Northern community life and business. The building of his new business premises, the Cochrane block, received practically blow-by-blow coverage in the Sudbury press in 1894. On March 29, the *Sudbury Journal* reported that Cochrane had purchased a major local corner at Cedar and Durham. A week later, he was selling off the existing buildings and planning to tear down what he couldn't sell. On May 17 the *Journal* reported that the excavation had been completed and "a plentiful supply of good water found at a depth of 112 feet" in one corner of what would be the basement. On May 31: "The plans promise a building that would be an ornament to any town." June 14: "Brickwork well underway." October 11: "Mr. Frank Cochrane is moving his stock into his new block this week."

And on October 25, the *Journal*, in a you-are-there visit for its readers, said in its preamble: "When a business man displays the energy, enterprise and capital necessary to erect and successfully complete an establishment such as we are about to describe, we feel he is entitled to all the praise and publicity at our disposal, as well as a very liberal share of general patronage. . . ."

The description of the premises started with the basement. It worked its way through all the stock in the hardware and ironmongery on the first floor. Then to the doctors and lawyers who occupied second-floor offices along with Cochrane's tin-smith department. Finally to the large third-floor halls ("with the necessary dressing, cloak and ante-rooms") for meetings of the Masons and other societies in the town. In the *Journal* story everybody from the carpenter to the decorator got a credit line. The report, after putting the building's cost at about $12,000, concluded: "We trust he will not only have no reason to regret this large investment, but that his most sanguine expectations will be quadruplicated, for, with his able manager, Mr. Reid, and seven assistants, a large varied and carefully selected stock to work on, every facility seems available for doing the business he richly deserves."*

His direct entry into politics came when nominations to town council were made for the January 1896 elections. Frank Cochrane was one of eight councillor candidates nominated for McCormick Ward. He and another candidate, George Elliott, later tied to head the poll.

One fact was apparent in Frank Cochrane's political life in Sudbury from then on. Beginning with the moment he won election, he was no longer one of the favourite sons of the editor of the *Sudbury Journal*, James A. Orr.

Cochrane was Conservative, Orr Liberal. Cochrane was one of an 1896 new wave that swept all but two of the old council

---

*The business was forerunner of Cochrane-Dunlop Hardware Limited, a major retail and wholesale supplier across Canada, in new frontier towns in the North as well as in major cities. His grandson is president.

out of office—and one of these two old-guard survivors was James A. Orr. In the federal election later that year, the local Conservative candidate was J. B. Klock. Cochrane was one of his campaign workers. The Liberal aspirant was James Conmee. Orr was one of Conmee's campaign workers. A blizzard of anti-Klock letters, editorials, charges of slander, etc., echoed through the *Sudbury Journal*'s pages right up to election time, and even in reporting that Klock won by a 915 majority, Mr. Orr went on, darkly: "Of the means by which this large majority was received we need say nothing just now, as the matter will, in all probability, be ventilated in the courts." (It was not.)

Cochrane and Orr met again the following January, head on, for the mayoralty. Cochrane won by an 18-vote majority, and probably only a politician can understand exactly the nature of the journalistic eye that Orr kept on the mayor from then on, through his news columns and editorial pages. This aspect was accentuated a year later when the two once again ran for mayor. Cochrane won easily, 185 votes to 44, causing Orr to start his report on the election results with the rather dispirited, "It is useless at the present time to discuss all the reasons which contributed to give Mayor Cochrane such a large majority, but . . . we believe that a large number of electors will be convinced before they are many moons older that they made a mistake. . . ."

The political career had been launched. It continued in the normal, fairly low-key manner of municipal politics: visits to the provincial government in Toronto to seek aid for this or that, chairing public meetings when issues of the day were debated, petitioning for favourable tax decisions for local industries, visiting mines, battling over minor local issues. But there is evidence that the small-potatoes aspect of the municipal scene bored Frank Cochrane. When the next nominations day came around again at the end of 1898, he did not stand for office. Neither did J. A. Orr. T. J. Ryan, nominated by representatives of two families to become famous in Sudbury, A.

Fournier and D. Rothschild, won by acclamation. Frank Cochrane served as mayor for one more term, in 1902, for reasons that will be examined in the next chapter.

Meanwhile he kept his influence alive by membership on the Board of Trade—he had been its first president—and in various citizens' groups, and by working in provincial and federal elections. The Cochranes, even out of office, continued a custom that they had started years before. They held open house at home each Sunday evening, with a large roast of beef, enough for all comers. Discussions were largely centred in politics and on the North. The best-known people in town waded through mud in spring, dust in summer, and snow in winter to the Cochrane home to debate politics and the future of the North. Relatives—Cochranes from Quebec and Dunlaps from Pembroke—were occasional visitors, especially Silent Frank's brother-in-law, David A. Dunlap, a barrister and solicitor in Mattawa who had added mining and prospecting to his legal activities. Alice Cochrane was known as Al to her friends; the warm respect and friendship between her husband and her brother Dave pleased her. Years of close consultation between the two men on mining and other matters later provided legislature debaters with plenty of anti-Cochrane ammunition on charges of favouritism and undue influence.

CHAPTER TWO

One can only guess why the Cochranes, although well off, never owned a home in either Mattawa or Sudbury. In his first four years in Sudbury, from 1890 on, his income rose enough that he could build his own grand business block, but he still rented the family home.

There is a distinct possibility that Alice Cochrane simply resisted putting down roots in the rough frontier milieu (although her old home, Pembroke, with its log drives and wild rivermen, wasn't exactly the heart's-core of genteel living either). Her first son, Wilbur, recalled her as a strong woman. Silent Frank, with his big and robust physique, was a known power all through the North, but at home, his son said, "His word was not necessarily law—far from it." At any rate, the schools in the North at the time were not the best. Cochrane concurred in the decision to send Wilbur to Toronto to attend Upper Canada College. When the time came for the younger children to enter high school a much more drastic arrangement was made. The Cochranes bought their first home and it was in Toronto, at 15 Maple Avenue, in the then newish Rosedale district just above Bloor Street, which not long previously had been the north city limit. Many fashionable families who had resided on Sherbourne and Jarvis streets in the last years of the nineteenth century by then had moved to Rosedale. The Cochrane family took over its new home in October 1900.

Five or six years previously, Cochrane had visited Toronto frequently, often on municipal business. Many times his wife went along to shop at the newly burgeoning Eaton's department store and to visit theatres. Now, although Toronto became their family home, for business and political reasons Frank Cochrane still based himself in Sudbury. A little needling grin might have crossed James A. Orr's face about then when he inserted a deadpan item in his *Journal*: "Mrs. F. Cochrane, of Toronto, is visiting friends in the district."

The evidence is that by 1901 Cochrane already had decided to broaden his political horizons. He was trying to influence Ontario Tory policy. On February 16, 1900, his name first appears in the papers of James Pliny Whitney, the Conservative who then was Ontario Opposition leader. Cochrane and R. R. Gamey, a controversial provincial member for Manitoulin, signed a letter to Whitney opposing an issue of the time: whether an export tax should be put on unrefined nickel, to force the building of a refinery in Canada. On March 15, 1901, Cochrane wrote more forcefully to Whitney. His tone suggested a strong commitment to provincial politics. He was against any export tax on nickel ore on the grounds that it would ruin, or severely hinder, Sudbury's major industry. "Of course, you know best what is in the best interest of our party and which action will bring you the most votes," he wrote, "but let me say that you knock your warmest supporters here on the head so that we will not be able to put up the fight that we have been working so hard for since 1898, to win Nipissing for you in the next election." He went on in similar vein before concluding: "Pardon me for writing at such length but feel it my duty to enter my protest with my leader."

Later that year, after the nickel export tax idea had been

dropped, and more correspondence with Whitney about the provincial election expected soon, Cochrane made a move that was perhaps calculated to bring him back into day-by-day prominence in district politics. Since his earlier years as mayor he had been more visible as a hardware and timber operator, with some mining and electric-power interests. But late in 1901 he turned up at the nominations meeting for the municipal elections. In those days, the nominations meeting was usually the biggest one of the municipal campaign.

The hall was packed. Everybody made a speech. This time the crowd saw a different Frank Cochrane. Nominated for mayor, he launched into a fiery speech in which he said that it appeared the present council wanted to stay in power forever, and the citizens were paying dearly for the honour. The financial statement was the worst he had ever seen. It was time to stop overdrafts at the bank. The electric light should be put on a businesslike basis (private customers paid 60 cents per light, business 66 2/3, and the town lost money).

Editor J. A. Orr moved out of political retirement at precisely the same time. Cochrane, to him, was like a red rag to a bull. Orr allowed his name to stand for mayor once again. In reporting the election results a week or so later for his *Journal* he wrote, "some influences were at work beyond our control. . . . A number of false and malicious reports were circulated. . . ." In short, the mayoralty results were Cochrane 205, Orr 64.

With that re-establishing victory under his belt, Cochrane worked hard in Sudbury in the next three months to show a record of achievement. Then the expected Ontario election was called by Liberal Premier G. W. Ross and Cochrane agreed to stand for the Conservative nomination. He was then nearly fifty years old, an imposingly tall and erect figure, with vertical lines down his face that gave him an appearance of sternness. He was known as a good mayor. But it didn't help at all with the French-Canadian majority in the constituency that he was a Methodist. His family's move to Toronto was a lesser factor because his business headquarters and he himself remained in Sudbury.

He had the unanimous support of the official Conservatives, the back-room boys, in the constituency. When a convention was held in Sudbury in April to select a candidate for West Nipissing, only Cochrane's name was put forward by the collection of political insiders on hand. They were mostly present or former federal or provincial members, along with a scattering of local politicians from Sturgeon Falls, Verner, Warren, Copper Cliff, and Sudbury. This business done, the meeting was adjourned for a few hours and then re-opened for speech-making, band selections, and generally exhorting the 450 persons present to sweep Cochrane into office. The bow to the French-Canadian majority in the constituency that year was in the form of electing one O. Aubin of Sturgeon Falls as the constituency association president. In Aubin's speech, he spoke some passages in French. To a predominantly French-Canadian electorate, that couldn't have seemed very over-whelming, especially as the Liberals had nominated a man who seemed to fit the constituency precisely, a French-Canadian Roman Catholic, Joseph Michaud.

The nature of electioneering in those days may be drawn from an item in Orr's *Sudbury Journal* for May 8, 1902, headed "Conservative Demonstration". Obviously both federal and provincial Tories were out in full war-paint, touring the constituencies to support local candidates and drum up local enthusiasm. The item read:

> The Conservatives of this place had a most successful demonstration on Tuesday, the occasion being the visit of Mr. J. P. Whitney, leader of the Opposition, accompanied by A. Carscallen, Hamilton; Col. Matheson, Perth; J. J. Foy, Dr. Pyne and Thos. Crawford, of Toronto—all members of the late Legislature; F. D. Monk, leader of the Quebec Conservatives in the Dominion House; Geo. McCormick, M.P., Muskoka, and J. B. Klock, ex-M.P. for Nipissing.

The party arrived by the Soo train and were met at the station by a large crowd of spectators. A procession was formed, headed by Copper Cliff Band and followed in rear by the Citizens' Band. All marched by way of Larch, Durham and Elm streets to the square where an address to Mr. Whitney was read and briefly responded to by Messrs. Whitney and Monk. The party was then escorted to the Balmoral Hotel for dinner. During the afternoon a reception was held in Lennon's Hall, and a large number of citizens were presented to the visitors.

Messrs. Pyne and Foy, accompanied by Mr. Cochrane, visited the schools and the children were given a holiday until the next day at noon.

Special trains were run from Cartier, on the main line, and from Webbwood, on the Soo line, and brought a large number of visitors.

A mass meeting was held at night in Lennon's Hall, which was completely filled, about 900 being present, including the largest number of ladies [who had no vote] ever seen at a political meeting here. The hall was handsomely decorated with flags and mottoes appropriate to the occasion. The Citizens' Band and Copper Cliff Band were present and rendered several selections during the evening. Mr. J. H. Clary presided. On the platform, in addition to the visitors named above were Mr. F. Cochrane, candidate for West Nipissing; Mr. W. R. Smyth, candidate in Algoma; Dr. Fell of Gore Bay, Mr. C. Lamarche of Mattawa and Mr. S. Fournier.

Mr. Cochrane was the first speaker. He was followed by Messrs. Smyth, Monk, Whitney, Foy, Carscallen, Fell and Matheson. Mr. Whitney received a great ovation, the C. C. Band playing, "He's a jolly good fellow." He was suffering from a severe cold but spoke for 55 minutes. [Causing one to reflect on the durability that would have been necessary in any audience which caught him in good health.]

It was near 12 o'clock when the meeting broke up with cheers for the King, Mr. Whitney and the candidate, Mr. Cochrane. The visitors left by Soo train the following day for Thessalon.

That seems to have been the first time that James Pliny Whitney and Frank Cochrane appeared on a platform together. They had ample opportunity to speak at length as the high Tory safari swept through the North, while Cochrane campaigned in his own straightforward style, covering a lot of ground and touching all the bases. A few weeks later the Liberals were returned to office, although with a sharply reduced majority. Two lines of newspaper type ended this phase of Frank Cochrane's political career:

> May 29, 1902.
> Ontario elections. West Nipissing. Mr. Michaud elected.

The 1902 meetings between Cochrane and Whitney were not wasted. Whitney had more and more opportunities to see Cochrane in Toronto. They came to be good friends. Both were shrewd politicians. They talked many times of Cochrane's defeat in West Nipissing in 1902. One conclusion was that there was just too much in the way of religion and racial background for a Methodist to buck in that largely French-speaking constituency.

Naturally, politicians who make deals do not usually leave elaborate memoranda behind for the guidance of the curious in later years. But the fact is that in the 1905 election, with Cochrane's support, Aubin—the token French-Canadian from the 1902 campaign—succeeded him as candidate in the West Nipissing nomination, and won. Charles Lamarche accepted the East Nipissing nomination and won.

In the campaign Whitney had hammered away at a point he'd often made in legislative debate: that the vast northern lands of Ontario should be represented in the cabinet. The custom then was to call the land from Pembroke to the Lakehead, New Ontario. "These thousands of square miles of our Ontario heritage might not have many people, because it is of course still a frontier, calling for the strongest and most robust of settlers," he declaimed. "But when so much of the province's present income is derived from logging and there is just now beginning of promise of mining riches beyond our dreams, it is a crime against the brave people in those districts that they have no one to speak for them in the councils of government. . . ." He said that if he were elected his government would have at least one minister from New Ontario.

He *was* elected, and immediately seemed to be facing one big problem: fulfilling that promise to put a Northerner in his cabinet. He had two or three men in mind, but two had not contested the election and the third had been beaten.

His solution was a secret at the time. Some aspects were revealed much later in a paper by Brian D. Tennyson.* His account was based on the Hearst and Whitney papers in the Ontario Archives.

> Whitney had tried to get Hearst [a resident of Sault Ste. Marie] to accept a nomination with the promise of a cabinet portfolio, as early as 1904. Upon his success at the polls in 1905, Whitney called in Hearst and Frank Cochrane—neither of whom had sought election—and told them that one of them had to enter his cabinet as a representative of Northern Ontario. They were given until the next morning to decide between them which it would be. As Hearst later told the story: "Mr. Cochrane and I spent that night until the early hours of the next morning trying to do what! Each trying to persuade the other that it was his duty to accept the position. Mr. Cochrane consented, but not before he had exacted from me a promise that I would seek election at the next general election and in time relieve him as Minister for Northern Ontario."

The situation might not have been quite that precise. Hearst's son, William, said in Toronto in 1970 that his father declined Whitney's invitation to enter politics in 1904 and 1905 because he was then a struggling young lawyer with a family to raise, and felt he could not afford the interruption to his career. Also, in a letter Hearst wrote to Whitney two days after the

*"The Succession of William H. Hearst to the Ontario Premiership—September, 1914", *Ontario History*, September, 1964.

election, he suggested "to your serious consideration the question of taking W. R. Smyth into the cabinet as Minister of Mines". He went on for one hundred words or so to extol Mr. Smyth, who had won Algoma East. Smyth later complained to Whitney when Cochrane was given this post. Whitney replied in a placating fashion but also said flatly: "... before the elections took place I had made up my mind to secure Mr. Cochrane for that position if possible.... It is my duty to try to get a man from New Ontario at once able and capable and who had also the necessary knowledge and experience for such a position. I believe I have succeeded."

Given the habit of politicians of not revealing all of the processes by which they reach decisions, it still seems that either Hearst was not privy to Whitney's full thoughts on the matter, or that after the fact, Whitney thought there was no point in admitting that he ever had thought of any cabinet candidate from the North but Cochrane.

All this, including the choice of Cochrane, was secret until the appointment was made late in May. But there were hints. It turned out that the victorious Charles Lamarche in East Nipissing had intended sitting as a Tory member only if the *Liberal* government was returned to office! The evidence was buried in a news item in the *Sudbury Journal* for February 2, 1905, eight days after the election.

CELEBRATION

The Conservatives of West Nipissing celebrated in town Thursday evening last; Mr. Aubin, the member elect, accompanied by a large number of friends from Sturgeon Falls and intermediate points, arrived here about 7 o'clock on No. 117. On their arrival a torchlight procession was formed, headed by the Sturgeon Falls Band, and paraded the principal streets, finally ending at the New American Hotel.

There was a plentiful supply of fireworks and the utmost enthusiasm prevailed. After supper the majority of the party spent an hour at the carnival, afterwards

adjourning to the Opera House. At the latter place
speeches were made ...

*In the course of his remarks Mr. Geo. Gordon said
that during the campaign in East Nipissing he had met
Mr. Chas. Lamarche, Conservative candidate, and the
latter told him that if he carried the constituency* (and
the Conservatives carried the province) *he proposed
resigning in favor of Mr. F. Cochrane whom he wished
to see a Cabinet Minister.* [Italics added.]

Mr. Cochrane, rising to speak a moment later, said
Mr. Gordon's remarks came to him as a great surprise.
He was not looking for a seat in the Cabinet, as he
thought ninety per cent of those elected to support
Mr. Whitney were better qualified than he was ...

There can be legitimate doubt that Cochrane was telling
all he knew on the subject when he uttered his disclaimer. But
old newspaper clippings are frail vessels of communication.
Perhaps this one omitted to mention a wink or a smile that could
have allowed Silent Frank to let his audience know that there
might be more to his denial than met the eye. In the same copy
of the *Journal* for February 2 was another item, an editorial
possibly prompted by the broad hint dropped by George Gordon.
The *Journal*, not notably a supporter of Cochrane, still
commented:

There is a strong feeling in this place both among
Mr. F. Cochrane's political friends and many who are
opposed to him, that he should receive the appointment of Minister of Mines in the Whitney Cabinet. It
is conceded that the office should be given to a New
Ontario man, and there are none of the elected Conservative members from New Ontario as well qualified
to fill the position as Mr. Cochrane. True he has no
seat, but that is a matter which can easily be arranged.
The office has not yet been established nor can it be until
after the new government has got into working order.
Mr. Cochrane has been a resident of Sudbury for
fourteen years, and a most successful merchant and
business man. He has been considerably interested in

mining also, and therefore has a practical knowledge of what is needed.

If the position is to be given to a New Ontario man, and it should be, we submit that there are none better qualified to fill the position than our townsman.

There was a third item about Frank Cochrane in that same issue. It was on the front page. It takes news of some significance to break up a front page to get a new item in, but the *Journal* was well into its final and completed form for the week when this news happened. A hasty check by telephone caused part of the front page to be cleared for this item:

ACCIDENT TO MR. COCHRANE

Mr. Frank Cochrane of this place met with a very serious accident today. Returning from the east on the Soo train, he got off at Wahnapitae station for a few minutes. As the train started to pull out he slipped at the steps of the first-class car, the wheel running over his right leg below the knee. With great presence of mind he caught the chain under the car, and was dragged over fifty yards before the train was stopped. The assistant doctor on the C.P.R. Sudbury-Toronto line bound up the limb, and Mr. Cochrane was taken through to Copper Cliff, to the Hospital there. The accident took place about 12:45, the train being over an hour late. General sympathy was expressed on all sides when the news was received here.

A telephone message from the Hospital, as we go to press, informs us that his right leg had been amputated between the ankle and knee. The left foot is also slightly injured.

One can only guess, with the help of a few meagre newspaper reports, at the repercussions of this accident. Whitney was counting on Cochrane for a cabinet post, and a particular one. The legislature was about to be called. It seems certain that the arrangement all along had been for Charles Lamarche to be simply a stand-in—a French-Canadian Roman Catholic who could win and then vacate the seat for Cochrane if Whitney won the province. If no accident had occurred Lamarche would have made his grand gesture immediately and Whitney in his new role as premier would have announced quickly to the public that Ontario's first Minister for the North had been chosen.

As Cochrane lay in hospital in Copper Cliff with his right leg gone below the knee he had many visitors, among them emissaries from Whitney. There were no telephones in hospital rooms in those days, but verbal messages and letters were passed back and forth. The agreement after the first few days was to do nothing for a while, until Cochrane's condition advanced enough to make a long-term decision. Meanwhile, the newspapers kept the public informed:

> March 9, 1905—Mr. F. Cochrane has made such good progress towards recovery from his recent accident that he will be able to go to his home in Toronto tonight. Supt. Brady's private car has been sent up from North Bay for Mr. Cochrane's use, so that he will be able to make the trip in comparative comfort.

In Toronto during the next two weeks Cochrane received three letters, totalling about 2,500 words, from his brother-in-law David Dunlap. The first indicated that Cochrane was still unsure about what to do: "You don't want, for certain reasons, the Portfolio that appears to be yours if you so choose." Dunlap admitted that Cochrane's business interests would suffer, perhaps disastrously, in his absence, but in two subsequent letters set forth in detail measures he urged Cochrane to take immediately he became mines minister. There was strong personal interest in this. Dunlap and his partners felt they had been done out of a rich claim, and, referring to the government official who had made the ruling, Dunlap wrote: "I could have shot him in his tracks if I had been within reach."

> April 13, 1905—Mr. Frank Cochrane's numerous friends here are pleased to see him back again in town, having arrived by noon train Saturday, accompanied by Mrs. Cochrane. The amputated limb has almost entirely healed, and Mr. Cochrane suffers but little pain.

This either was a miraculous recovery, or Cochrane was playing down the pain. Actually the leg bothered him for the rest of his life.

> May 4, 1905—Mr. F. Cochrane left for Toronto Friday evening, and will go to New York for the purpose of being fitted with a cork foot.

During the two months after the train accident, and especially in the last weeks of April, an understanding was reached between Cochrane and Whitney. The accident would postpone, not cancel, their political plans. But the legislature was in session and pressures were growing on the premier to create a mines department (there was none) and appoint a strong man as mines minister, to cope with the mining boom then under way around Cobalt.

One major argument already had developed, the one to which David Dunlap had referred. There was a strong political tinge here in that the Renfrew millionaire M. J. O'Brien, a bearded, big man who was one of the principal railroad contractors of the time, had acquired title to some claims near Cobalt on the Temiskaming and Northern Ontario Railway at a time when he was a commissioner of the T. and N. O., an indisputable Liberal political appointment. He had picked up the claims from a prospector named Neil King for a few thousand dollars, and the Liberal government of Premier Ross had approved the O'Brien title. But meanwhile David Dunlap's powerful group, in which he was allied with Noah and Henry Timmins and Duncan and John McMartin, was charging that the O'Brien claims had been dishonestly staked in the first place by Neil King, and that the real owner was a blacksmith named Fred LaRose—from whom the Timmins-McMartin-Dunlap group had bought some of the same property claimed by O'Brien.

The O'Brien title to the claims had been signed by the Commissioner for Crown Lands in Ontario early in February, in effect giving Conservative government approval on top of the previous Liberal government approval. However, the rights and wrongs of the conflict were still being fought in the press and elsewhere. It was the kind of hot potato that no new minister particularly needs; especially a minister whose wife's brother is one of the disputants.

Pressure increased for a department of mines that would produce a coherent policy governing claims, and take mining affairs out from under the existing Crown Lands commissioner whose main functions had been with logging, the principal factor in the Northern Ontario economy of the time.

In mid-May the first open signs of action came when Whitney rose in the legislature to introduce a bill creating a new department to be known as President of the Council. He would take this position himself, he said. Mr. Foy, who was Commissioner of Crown Lands, would become Attorney General. Instead of a separate Department of Mines being created, Crown Lands and Mines would be combined. The official in charge would be a minister instead of a commissioner. The changes left the office of Minister of Crown Lands and Mines vacant, and, reported the press, "There are persistent rumours that Mr. F. Cochrane of Sudbury will receive the appointment." The name of William Hearst of the Sault was also mentioned. The *Sudbury Journal* again gave the opinion that Mr. Cochrane was best suited for the position because "he ... is well acquainted with a large section of New Ontario, and has been more in touch and identified with mining interests than any of the other candidates mentioned." Editor Orr, with uncharacteristic restraint, did not mention that one of the "interests" included a brother-in-law.

The legislature was prorogued May 26. Three days later Cochrane was named Minister of Crown Lands and Mines and was shown to his new office in the southeast corner of the Legislative Building's main floor by Premier Whitney. One of the rare first-hand accounts of that day, beginning Cochrane's ministerial career, was recalled in 1950 by his long-time secretary, George Yates, who was then in his seventy-eighth year and retired in Ottawa. "He entered the office on crutches," Mr. Yates wrote. "And that was the occasion of our first meeting. As a member of the staff of The Globe for six years before, and a reporter for that paper in the Legislative Press Gallery, I had been appointed private secretary to the Commissioner of Crown Lands under the [A.S.] Hardy government in 1899. [This was just before Hardy resigned his seat and the premiership, in favour of George W. Ross.] Mr. Cochrane was kind enough to invite me to continue in that position when he became minister. For a Conservative minister to take over the private secretary of his Liberal predecessor was a unique event at that time, particularly so in view of the political animosities aroused in the protracted struggle of the Conservatives to attain power after the thirty-third year of Liberal tenure just ended. However, I mention it merely to show that Mr. Cochrane, though a staunch Conservative and a man of strong political convictions, was nevertheless devoid of the narrow partisanship so often displayed in the matter of political appointments."

Cochrane was sworn in on May 30 at Queen's Park. The legislature of those days met only for a few months each spring, so he would have eight months or so before he would have to face that side of his job, the debating society, the role that suited him least. After the ceremony, the normally acerbic Premier Whitney was more than usually out-giving to the press. He said that the appointment had been delayed by the accident to Mr. Cochrane but that now things would proceed rapidly. Charles Lamarche had resigned to open the seat of East Nipissing, he said. Nominations would be June 13 with a by-election one week later, June 20. The writs for the by-election already had been issued in East Nipissing. Whitney denied with some heat that any arrangement had been made to reward Lamarche for his resignation by giving him some other government appointment.

The *Toronto Star*, in its news columns, summarized Mr.

Cochrane's background and presumably went to work digging into that background without delay. Criticism of the appointment began in the *Star* a day or two later.

Immediately after his swearing-in, Cochrane boarded the Soo line train for Sudbury to organize his election campaign. Efforts, which were to become a political embarrassment three years later, were being made to persuade East Nipissing Liberals that they stood to gain more by allowing his acclamation than by opposing the first New Ontario minister ever appointed. Meanwhile, a fair-sized storm broke in the Toronto newspapers over the appointment.

The Toronto dailies then were the mighty *Globe* (Liberal), the struggling new *Star* (Liberal), the *Evening Telegram* (Independent but mainly Conservative), the *World* (Conservative), the *Mail and Empire* (Conservative), and the *News* (Independent with Conservative leanings). They lined up fairly accurately according to party lines, except for the *Telegram*, whose view was confused by another issue, that Cochrane's constituency was largely French-Canadian and Roman Catholic. The *Telegram* did not care at all for this combination's being represented in cabinet, even by a Methodist.

The *Globe*, in an editorial headed "Hon. Frank Cochrane", said that in carrying out the promised reconstruction of his cabinet to include a minister from the North the Premier had acted wisely for both himself and the province. But:

> The Premier has taken an unusual, if not an unnecessary, risk in selecting as administrator of this department a gentleman who has never been in Parliament, and has never won for himself any wide-spread prominence in any other sphere of activity. To the people of the locality in which he lives he is well and favorably known but it is a new departure of a serious kind to appoint a gentleman without legislative experience to the most important portfolio in the Government. Mr. Cochrane might conceivably be the best head the department has ever had, and might nevertheless

prove a failure as a Minister because of Parliamentary ineptitude. Under our system of responsible government each member of the Executive Council of the Province must be a Parliamentarian as well as an administrator, and if the new Minister of Lands and Mines fails in the former capacity he will fail altogether.

Mr. Cochrane has been identified in business with both the lumbering and the mining industry, and it is urged in explanation of his appointment that his practical acquaintance with them gives him special fitness for the portfolio which has been assigned to him. It will be hard to convince the public that this kind of reasoning is not fallacious, in view of the traditional practice (unbroken since Confederation) of entrusting the administration of the public domain to a trained and practical lawyer. . . . Some of the most important functions of the Minister of Lands and Mines are quasi-judicial, and if the incumbent of the office is not himself a trained jurist, he must needs depend very frequently on the advice furnished by others. Such a necessity does not make for promptitude in the work of administration.

If, as common report alleges, Mr. Cochrane is financially interested in either timber berths or mining locations, he may find it difficult to convince other operators that his administration is perfectly impartial, and the general public that his policy is above suspicion. . . . Mr. Cochrane may prove to be a "find", and may amply justify Mr. Whitney's choice, but the facts that are known to the general public do not support it.

The *Telegram* was blunter, for its own reasons. Under the heading "Mr. Whitney's Mistake", the *Telegram* said:

A minister whose political life is at the mercy of the race and creed prejudice of an overwhelmingly French-Canadian constituency can add no strength to the Whitney Government.

French-Canadianism is sufficiently represented by the presence of Hon. Dr. Reaume in the Ontario Government, and a Minister who is at the mercy of the French-Canadian whims of East Nipissing must be a remarkable man if he does not prove to be a weakness to Hon. J. P. Whitney.

The English-Canadian public man who owes his political life to French-Canadians must always be more extreme in his deference to their racial and religious prejudices than the French-Canadian public man who has his English-speaking constituents to consider.

There seems to be no good reason why two portfolios should be allotted to the handful of French-Canadian constituencies in this province. It will be a miracle if a public man whose legislative life is at the mercy of the French-Canadians of East Nipissing develops into an element of strength in the membership of the Ontario Government.

The Toronto *World* found nothing to carp about. Quite the contrary. It intoned in a long, advice-filled editorial:

The World is bound to believe that the selection is a wise one. . . .

But these were only the opening salvoes in what soon became a blistering barrage, building the Cochrane appointment into one of the most controversial items on the political scene of that time.

The *Globe* followed up its obvious editorial disapproval four days later with a long newspaper article date-lined Cobalt and headed: "Come Now, Mr. Cochrane! Did you wage battle for the nickel trust?"

Using the device of attributing the meat of the story to "special correspondence", the unsigned article stated that Cochrane's selection for his important and responsible position, "despite the availability of fitter men", was forced on the government by one of the banks. A further charge was that Cochrane was a tool of the big nickel interests in the Sudbury area. The anonymous writer recalled that in 1898 there was agitation in Ontario for an export duty on nickel ore and mattes, to benefit Canada by encouraging the nickel companies to move their refining operations to Canada.

The Toronto Board of Trade had appointed a special committee of its members to investigate the whole nickel question.

"The committee . . . published the conclusions they had arrived at: all in favour of having the nickel refined in this country. . . ."

> But in the meantime [wrote the *Globe*'s special correspondent] the Canadian Copper Company, or parent company of the nickel trust naturally opposed the imposition of an export duty on nickel ores and mattes, and here is where Frank Cochrane comes in, but not in a high or patriotic aspect. A long circular letter, typewritten on foolscap paper, was got up at the head office of the Canadian Copper Company in Cleveland, and sent to the company's office at Copper Cliff to be revised and corrected there. It was a remarkable document when finished, and contained all sorts of misstatements of facts in regard to the nickel industry. But instead of being signed by the President of the company this circular letter was taken to Sudbury and signed by Frank Cochrane and fathered by him as the production of his own hand and brain! Not one but many copies of the letter were so signed by him, and sent to the Dominion Government and various Boards of Trade in Ontario. And the people of the Sudbury district knew only too well that it was done from a poor, narrow motive. The unpatriotic nature of this act, not to use a harsher term, ought to be a bitter recollection to the Hon. Frank Cochrane now. But is it?

There is no doubt, from Cochrane's earlier representations to Whitney on the matter, that he was against the export tax. No copy of the letter referred to by the *Globe*'s special correspondent has been found, or confirmation of its source or nature, as charged. However, there is one area of partial corroboration, as well as of possible confusion. At the time the letter was supposed to have been written, Cochrane was Sudbury's mayor. When the federal government of Sir Wilfrid Laurier was considering an export tax on nickel ore and mattes in 1898, the nickel industry was a major factor in Sudbury's existence and there was concern for the welfare of the town. A special meeting of the town council was called and a committee of three, Mayor Cochrane and Councillors Howey and Lemieux, was appointed to study the situation and draft a resolution to be sent to the Dominion Government.* The resolution opposed the tax, but not the idea of establishing a refinery in Canada. To establish an export tax before building a refinery would "be subversive to the best interests of the country and bring direct ruin and destitution upon many of the people of Sudbury."

It was moved and seconded that "the resolution be sent to

*The resolution approved by Sudbury Town Council:

WHEREAS the government of the Dominion of Canada has under contemplation the imposition of an export tax on nickel matte, and

WHEREAS there is not established in Canada at the present time any refining for the purposes of treating nickel ores, and

WHEREAS of the several companies who have been operating in the nickel mining in Canada in the last ten years all have closed their work with the exception of one, and

WHEREAS the continued operation of this one company has been of incalculable value to the whole country, and

WHEREAS the people of Sudbury and its vicinity are greatly dependant on the company for their employment, and

WHEREAS the company pays annually one-quarter of a million dollars in wages, and

WHEREAS the imposition of an export duty would prejudicially affect the said company and thereby jeopardize the welfare of our citizens as well as the prosperity of the Town,

THEREFORE, be it resoluted that the council of the Town of Sudbury, although not disapproving of the principle that Canada should reap the benefits of the refining and manufacture of her natural mineral resources, nevertheless under present existing circumstances whilst the nickel industry is only in its first stage of development and before any refineries are established and in operation in this country, consider that any restrictions would be subversive of the best interests of the country and bring direct ruin and destitution upon many of the people of a portion of the province of Ontario which would not be compensated for by any benefit which might be derived by any other portion of the dominion by the imposition of any export duties.

Sir Wilfrid Laurier, the Minister of Finance, the Minister of Trade and Commerce", and others. It was a custom at the time that such resolutions were sent far and wide to other municipalities, boards of trade, and other organizations from which support might be forthcoming. In such cases Cochrane would show as one of the signatories and it is possible that his covering letter fitted the description later given by the *Globe*.

The *Globe*'s obviously partisan attack, however, apparently fell as quietly as a feather into the well-ordered arrangements for Cochrane to enter the legislature from East Nipissing. Cochrane had told Whitney in a letter that he hoped the Liberals would not contest the by-election. Some factors in how the Liberals were helped to reach this decision did not become public until another election brought mud-slinging three years later. But Cochrane was unopposed, elected by acclamation.

"East Nipissing Gladly Returns New Minister", swooned the *Mail and Empire* headline over a report from North Bay that continued:

> East Nipissing honoured itself, and at the same time paid a graceful compliment to Premier Whitney's choice, when today (at a meeting in a packed theatre) it gave the unanimous nomination of both parties to the new Minister of Lands and Mines, Hon. Frank Cochrane. It was a remarkable tribute to him that Conservatives and Liberals alike should unite in selecting him as their representative in the Legislature, and the greatest of satisfaction is felt at the choice. . . .

Premier Whitney was on hand to help in the festivities. Early on in the program the packed theatre was treated to Charles Lamarche's explaining why he had resigned his seat. He had not been asked by Premier Whitney or anyone else to resign, he said. He simply felt that it would be a good thing for the riding if it were represented at Toronto by a cabinet minister. Premier Whitney had lots of men to choose from, but he had made a promise that he would take a man from New Ontario into his cabinet. Mr. Lamarche had recommended Mr. Cochrane for the position, and was extremely glad that he had secured it. The interests of East Nipissing would be well looked after by the new minister. (Applause, extending into an ovation.)

Cochrane was given a rousing reception when he rose to speak. He was a very proud man, he said, because Mr. Whitney had selected him as Minister of Lands and Mines, and because East Nipissing had elected him unanimously as their representative. (Not a bad parlay, as Lamarche had won it in January by only sixty-three votes.) He had not sought the position, on the contrary the position had sought him, and he was pleased to accept it. The duties of the office would be discharged to the best of his ability.

"I want every elector of this riding," said Mr. Cochrane, "irrespective of country, religion or politics, to feel that I am their representative and will do my best to look after their interests." (Applause.)

Premier Whitney was greeted with loud cheers and proceeded to speak for more than an hour, strewing compliments, jokes, promises, jibes at Liberals, and reflections on the current scene before his fascinated audience:

> And I will say right here that speaking as the Premier of Ontario, I am proud to stand here today and acknowledge what the Province of Ontario owes to Charles Lamarche. (Cheers.)
>
> There were people who tried to stir up strife and ill feeling in Canada [he went on]. . . . There were different races and creeds in the country, but its record since Confederation was one which they need not feel ashamed of. Almost forty years had elapsed since Confederation and would it not be strange if in all that time no ripple appeared on Canada's sea of contentment? Would it not be strange if in that time there had not been some political and mental dyspepsia? But in all those years the people had kept before them the idea that they were living under the benign wing of Providence, where every man worshipped according to the dictates of his own conscience.

The exalted statesmanship shown by Mr. Lamarche and his compatriots in standing by Mr. Cochrane would never be forgotten, and East Nipissing, by its action, had given an answer which would go all over Canada, and be a warning to demagogues and others of that ilk, that there was no place for them in this country. (Cheers.)

However, a slightly less romantic light was cast on the whole proceeding a few weeks later when the Toronto *World* reported from Mattawa that the reason the Liberals did not oppose Cochrane in the by-election lay in a deal local Liberal party officials had made with Cochrane. Reported the *World*:

> Someone wrote to the executive of the Reform Association of the riding, proposing a "saw-off", the arrangement being that, if Mr. Cochrane were given the seat without a contest the government would not dismiss any of the officeholders in New Ontario, "except for cause." This was given a wide meaning, and the Reform executive thought they were making a good bargain in agreeing to the saw-off, thus protecting a horde of officials [who were Liberal supporters and had received their jobs through Liberal patronage].
>
> Though there have been a few insignificant changes, the Conservatives of the northern districts have come to believe that the government is going to make good its compact with the East Nipissing Liberals. This belief is causing a tremendous howl throughout the north, not only because there are hundreds of Conservatives who are anxious to secure these comfortable berths, but because Mr. Whitney and his associates, when in opposition, were justly indignant about the actions of these same officials . . . calling them partisans of the rankest type, and saying that New Ontario was being stunted because of their unjust acts.

"There is not a word of truth in the story," said Cochrane in Toronto the next day. There was no communication with the Reform Association, he said, "and there was no understanding whatever that I was to secure the seat without a contest on condition that officials appointed by the late government should not be dismissed." (This statement was not openly challenged until three years later in the next campaign.) All the same, politics of the time being what they were, a month or two later Charles Lamarche, whose selflessness had been lauded so colourfully by everyone up to and including the Premier, was named a magistrate to replace a Liberal, John Loughrin. Loughrin had been fired for what was called "offensive political partisanship". He had been appointed in 1902 after losing an election, a simple patronage appointment that is not unknown even today for defeated candidates. But the custom of the time was that if a man wished to hold such a job indefinitely, he could not openly campaign later for the party that had put him there. Loughrin had broken that rule by running for office in the January election—and he couldn't very well run without making plain what party he stood for. "Offensive political partisanship!" It was handy for the Conservatives, giving them a place for Charles Lamarche at slightly more pay than the $1,000 he would have received as a private member of the legislature.

CHAPTER THREE

The Toronto in which Frank Cochrane became a well-known
and controversial figure in 1905 was rather a becoming setting
for any tall, straight, and stern man who wore high, stiff
collars, and spats—yet had links in the mines and woods of the
North. Premier Whitney and many other members stayed at
the old Queen's Hotel, where the Royal York now stands. One
of the favourite dining places was the Victoria Room of the
King Edward Hotel. In the opinion of Eric Arthur, in his book
Toronto, No Mean City, "modern architecture in Toronto has
so far failed to produce a hotel dining room with anything like
the flair and gaiety of this one." Legendary deals, both political and commercial, were made by the substantial men who sat
around the hotel's lobby and lunched or dined under the
magnificent decorative plaster work of the Victoria Room's
high ceiling. There were still many carriages on the streets,
mingling with horse-drawn delivery wagons from retailers and
wholesalers and a growing number of automobiles and electric
trolley-cars. These, not long before, had replaced the old
horse-drawn variety of public transportation—cars that looked
like tiny streetcars, drawn usually by one team, although snow-
ploughs of the period might be drawn by as many as ten horses.

The downtown area only a few years earlier had come under the domination of the Toronto City Hall with its gargoyle-trimmed clock tower.

The route that Frank Cochrane customarily walked or rode to his office at Queen's Park (he was now fairly comfortable with his artificial leg) was typical of the newer parts of the city. The busy streets in front of the massive homes in the upper Jarvis Street area were flanked by wide grassy boulevards and tall elms and maples. Then for a few blocks there were much more modest houses and businesses. But when he came nearer to the legislative buildings the homes were of imposing size again. Even the ornate stone stables behind some of these showed the architectural influence of the time. When Frank Cochrane reached the grounds of Queen's Park and stood at the main entrance, looking south along University Avenue, the sight was of an already impressive city. Tall spires of churches rose through the blanket of trees. Carriages with their coachmen sitting high rattled north and south on University Avenue, a street then wide enough for about three carriages abreast but not much more. Women in bustled dresses that skimmed the ground strolled with their children on paved walks through the wide lawns in front of the legislature.

Turning from that scene, Frank Cochrane would enter the massive main rotunda and turn right to his office. He did not demand that his secretary, George Yates, and other office staff arrive as early as he did, but his own devotion to long hours at his desk was mentioned in almost everything written about him at that time, even by his detractors.

The architecture of the legislative buildings is not generally considered to be of the highest standard, but, built of the same red sandstone as the 1899 City Hall, from a quarry near the forks of the Credit River, they had an interior grace and spaciousness that fitted an Ontario already bustling toward its position as a prime mover of Canadian affairs.

It seems almost incredible, in today's terms, to contemplate what was to become the main contribution Frank Cochrane would make to Ontario: to help frame and then battle through into law, against fierce opposition, a Mining Act that would allow the people of Ontario to share in the profits of mineral resources. This right is taken for granted today, when it is much better realized that Ontario's north is blessed with mining riches on a scale found in few other parts of the world. The Canadian Shield, product of a prehistoric upheaval of the earth's crust following the corrosion of the Ice Age, runs from Newfoundland and Labrador through Quebec and Northern Ontario and across the prairies to a small corner of Alberta. It also covers much of the Northwest Territories and parts of the Canadian Arctic Archipelago. Mining along the Shield in Quebec began twenty years before Confederation, and ore was first noticed at about the same period in Ontario. During Geological Survey of Canada work in the period from 1848 on, there were frequent reports of iron, nickel-cobalt, arsenic, sulphur, and copper, but there were no transportation facilities to make commercial mining practical until the railroad began to push through in the early 1880s. From then on the finds came thick and fast, some being made by active prospectors but others by persons who simply noticed the presence of ore in rock ballast being hauled for the Canadian Pacific Railway right-of-way. In the 1880s it wasn't even necessary to stake a claim. As D. M. LeBourdais wrote in his book *Sudbury Basin,* "most of the territory about Sudbury was already surveyed into townships and lots, and all the prospector need do was to locate the lot he wished to acquire and make application to the Department of Crown Lands at Toronto. The application was usually accompanied by an affidavit that the applicant, or his agent, had found what seemed to be a mineral deposit, but this was not always required."

By the mid-1880s, many new prospectors were arriving to scour the Sudbury region and by 1890 the area was dotted with real finds, most of them waiting only the much greater outlay of capital required to develop them as mines. The activity became so great that in 1892 Ontario passed its first Mines

Act, which, in retrospect, was almost laughable in its modesty
—or seemed so, by the time Frank Cochrane started his
labours at Queen's Park. Its provisions presumably suited the
early 1890s but had fallen far behind the fifteen-year mining
boom that preceded Cochrane's joining the cabinet. The out-
dated laws provided that anyone could explore Crown lands
for minerals. Mining lands could be taken up as surveyed
locations or as staked claims. The locations could run from 40
to 320 acres, with an initial cost running only to $3.50 an
acre, with rents of from 15 to 25 cents an acre after the first
year. Claims, which the law said had to be worked continuously, were rented at $1 an acre per year. Government
royalties on ores (the only meagre way the public shared the
exploitation of these natural resources) ran from two to three
per cent of the value at the pit's mouth, less cost of labour
and explosives—and royalty wasn't charged for the first seven
years in any case, or for the first fifteen years for anyone who
had been an original discoverer of ore or mineral.

Cochrane was scarcely in office before he was in the thick
of the new administration's initial attacks, mainly aimed at
big operators who had acquired leases on mining locations by,
as Attorney General J. J. Foy put it, "mistake and fraud".
The first three writs against mine operators were issued in July
and Cochrane told the *Mail and Empire* that they were the
first of a series to be investigated by the courts. In addition
to those cases that went to court, there were some in which
Cochrane was called upon personally to settle disputes—the
legal arguments presented to him by batteries of lawyers,
almost in a courtroom atmosphere.

In August, he was in the North to turn on the water supply
for the electrical power company that he and William
McVittie owned at Wahnapitae.* The *Kincardine Review*

*The Wahnapitae Power Company interest remained in the
Cochrane family until 1928, when his estate sold its share to
Ontario Hydro for $1,059,000. William McVittie held out for
another two years, then sold the balance to Hydro for $1,030,000.
McVittie died in 1933, aged 83.

chose this time to zero in on one of the major mining areas under dispute, that at Cobalt.

"Many of the claims are in dispute," the *Review* reported, and "the mining community are therefore in a state of unrest and uncertainty, but they have the utmost confidence in the Hon. Frank Cochrane. . . . He knows a good deal about mining, has plenty of energy, sound common sense, and superb courage. He put off his coat at Cobalt and tramped from claim to claim to examine the discoveries and interview the miners personally. Other members of the party tired out and went to the [railway] car, 'bushed' by a man who lost a leg only a few months ago . . . "

One of Cochrane's first major hearings was indicative of many to come. It was typical of what his administration had as its main target: to stop the custom of big operators blanketing an area with claims or leased locations, and then not working them, but waiting until something turned up, on the grounds that the more land a mining company had under lease, the better off it was. A. H. Beath of Sudbury had discovered that the Edison Exploration Company had blanketed a region but hadn't met the exploration provisions (which were scarcely policed at all at the time). Beath applied for the land and did comply with the Mines Act, whereupon the land was taken away from Edison and given to him. The company appealed, but Cochrane heard the appeal and upheld Beath.

The importance of Cochrane's part in the fight against boom tactics, in which some brokers were able to sell fake stock and injure honest development, was shown in mining incorporation figures: 1 in 1903, 4 in 1904, 43 in 1905, and 127 in 1906. (By late 1907, the number in Cobalt and Larder Lake alone had reached 500.) The broker-inspired boom of the summer of 1905 collapsed in the failure of several wildcat mining companies, and while this had lasting effects on the development of honest mining, the evidence that control was needed made Cochrane's activity much more acceptable to the general public—if not to the brokers. Cochrane's cooling-off policies, insisting that minerals be shown to exist before any company could be granted a title to its claim, contributed much to ending the artificial elements of the boom.

A complicated case that was to crop up again and again in subsequent years was that of the so-called Gillies Limits in the Cobalt country. Some big timber operators, the Gillies brothers of Arnprior, years earlier before the Cobalt discoveries, had licensed a large block of land for timber-cutting. Under the existing law, no one could prospect lands that were under timber licence. But this parcel was so close to the rich discoveries at Cobalt that many prospectors had moved in surreptitiously and staked claims, burying the stakes so that when the timber licence ended they would be able to claim they were first in the field. The *Globe* reported, indeed, "that practically all the limits in question have been staked out by prospectors, who have relied on the old adage that possession is nine points of the law. There are tales of buried claim stakes and mines of fabulous wealth belonging to men who only await the cutting of the timber to reveal their discoveries and become millionaires."

The *Globe* reporter on that story sought out Cochrane for comment. Cochrane was asked if he would say anything about the rights of the prospectors who had staked claims in the Gillies Limits.

"No," Cochrane replied.

End of interview.

While Cochrane busily went about cancelling leases, re-shuffling some jobs in his department, and conducting Premier Whitney on a tour of Cobalt and other mining areas where he hadn't been before, he also was at work on what was to become his major contribution to Ontario statutes: the new Mining Act.

On October 5, 1905, one of his attempts to make this act a generally acceptable one surfaced. He wrote to Crown lands agents throughout Ontario and asked them to call regional meetings at which mining men would be asked for their views on rewriting the present mining regulations. These meetings were held in Kingston, Madoc, Haileybury, Sudbury, Sault Ste. Marie, Port Arthur, Kenora, and Fort Frances. Each meeting was asked to appoint delegates to carry findings and recommendations to an Ontario-wide convention in Toronto in December. Meanwhile, Cochrane continued to tour the areas on his own fact-finding missions—and at almost every stop he was beset by mining men quizzing him on his intentions. In one such confrontation in Haileybury by members of the Mining Association there, the *Haileyburian* reported, "He stood his close cross-examination well; so well that men who thought earlier that he would be of no use are today compelled to give credit to Premier Whitney for the wisdom of his selection."

The December convention at which Cochrane sought advice on rewriting the Mining Act was less rewarding, even though it did produce one of the most comment-provoking keynote phrases of the entire Mining Act issue. Speaking to the convention on its first day at the King Edward Hotel, Cochrane stated flatly that in business affairs in the province, including mining, "Pull is dead."

This immediately became the text for a kidding editorial in the *Star*:

> "Pull is dead," announced Hon. Frank Cochrane in addressing the convention of mining men the other day. From the applause that the news occasioned it would seem that Pull had not a friend present. And yet—and yet, as we read the names of all those present it seems strange that were the news really true, nobody was carried fainting from the spot, or moaned as a sudden chill darted through bosoms warm with hopes.
>
> Is Pull dead? Is not the news of his death greatly exaggerated? If Mr. Cochrane should open the grave would he not find the coffin empty? As a matter of fact, you couldn't kill Pull. He is immortal. The only time when he was in the least danger was in Noah's flood, when the whole earth was covered with water. Dripping and alarmed, Pull survived and soon grew strong again.

Pull was not killed on election day in Ontario. He
merely removed his moustache, turned his coat, and
changed his boarding house.

If the impression can be created that he is dead,
this will suit his plans exactly—especially in mining
matters and with the great ripe fruit of the Cobalt
region to be plucked when spring opens, and Pull throbs
with new life. Pull is not dead. He is foxing. Several
people have seen and recognized him in the past
fortnight. . . . Nobody, we fancy, stands more in need
of keeping a sharp look-out for Pull than Hon. Frank
Cochrane. He has the job of his life ahead of him.

The convention ran four days at the King Edward. It
opened on a Tuesday with about a hundred men present,
but had dwindled to a few dozen by Friday. That day,
several members of the conference called at Queen's Park to
present the resolutions that had been passed. Mainly, they
dealt with arguments which often are still heard nearly seventy
years later: that increased taxation would kill the goose that
laid the golden egg, forcing miners and prospectors into other,
less restricted, lines of work. One resolution also asked that
the mines department should be separated from that of lands.
A few weeks earlier, Cochrane's enormous department had
been relieved of its division of Colonization and Forestry
(moved to Agriculture), but he told the mining men that it
was impossible to have a mines department separate from
lands. He seemed to have a point, as was well illustrated in
the case of the Gillies Limits where timber rights and prospecting rights were competing for attention. "The work is so
interwoven as to make separation impossible," Cochrane told
the mining industry representatives. "It would only lead to
troubles, squabbles and unnecessary delays." He already had,
he seemed to think, more than enough of those without courting more.

CHAPTER FOUR

There was obviously a careful method in Premier Whitney's decision not to swear in Frank Cochrane as Minister of Lands and Mines until after the end of the 1905 session. This gave him a clear eight months to take hold of his department before he had to face legislative debate on his policies. By the time the 1906 session was called in mid-February, many sections of the new Mining Bill had been threshed out in cabinet, although the whole bill did not clear cabinet until more than a month later. Also, bursting mining activity in the north had made essential a system of priorities that resulted in Cochrane's deciding to bring his reforms into effect in two stages. The first would be designed to bring order out of the chaotic staking and claiming practices. The second, which he decided would not be presented for another year, would deal with the revenues the government would demand of mining operations in the future.

The urgency of regulating control of mining claims also could be seen in an abrupt rise in mineral production in 1905. For several years previously mining production in Ontario had been around $11 or $12 million in aggregate output. In 1905 this figure rose to $19 million for the matte (an

unfinished product) or closer to $23 million when the re-
fined value was computed. The danger was that every week
that passed under the 1892 regulations perpetuated a system in
which the big mining operators could become entrenched in
situations that didn't jibe with the province's new protective
attitude toward the public's right to share in exploitation of
natural resources.

The bill was still very much under wraps when the session
began, but discussions in cabinet had spread knowledge about
its conditions among so many that leaks were inevitable. The
Toronto *World* published on February 20, nearly six weeks
before the bill was given first reading, a well-informed, if
sketchy, summary of it. The *London Free Press* had checked in
a day earlier with a similar speculative story. Editorial writers
on several papers began to take sides on the basis of the
speculative reports. In the legislature, Opposition members
pecked away trying to ferret out details, but one of the few
admissions they got from Silent Frank was on February 21,
when he told a questioner that the Gillies brothers had been
instructed in no uncertain terms that they were to clean up
all timber-cutting on their limits near Cobalt by October 1
and make way for the miners, who until then would be
barred from prospecting.

The *Globe*, which had been among the most critical of the
original Cochrane appointment, hailed this as a "wise arrangement" on two scores—protecting the public interest from both
the mining and the timber-cutting operators. "The government will be justified in making, at any reasonable expense,
the exclusion of prospectors as complete as possible," the
Globe wrote.

> It is quite impracticable to insure the safety of timber
> if prospectors are allowed to swarm over the territory,
> and to expose it to needless risk would be unfair to both
> the licensees, who have made payment in advance, and
> the public, who have a joint interest in the economic
> value of the timber crop. . . . Enough bush rangers with

constabulary powers should be appointed to arrest as trespassers all who are found at work on the forbidden ground. Any precautions less thorough would turn the prohibition into a farce. . . .

The Minister of Lands and Mines has announced that in disposing of the timber limit for mining purposes the most ample precautions will be taken to guard the interests of all parties, the public at large presumably included. Mr. Cochrane will find himself face to face with an extremely onerous and thankless task if he has to work under the present regulations. The affidavits of prospectors will descend in overwhelming showers on his devoted head and well for him if he does not lose it under the avalanche. These documents are not likely to be so veracious. Stakes will be surreptitiously removed, to be replaced by others. Disputes of all sorts will arise as to areas, boundaries, and priority. The Minister will have to decide these as best he can, but his decisions will not in all cases bar litigation. The whole district may be blanketed with law suits, and mining operations may be delayed indefinitely while the courts leisurely investigate titles and the lawyers energetically collect fees. Cobalt for the latter [the lawyers] will be better than a Klondike.

That seems to have been precisely what Frank Cochrane had in mind. He brought down the Mining Bill on March 29, and early in April it was given second reading. While some heckling came from the Opposition because revenue aspects of the new legislation would not be set forth for another year, there was general approval. In this, the legislature reflected a plain public satisfaction in what had been done.

One voter's letter to Whitney a day after the second reading said, "You have given thousands of us who never expected to have it in any other way, an interest in a silver mine. I congratulate you and your minister of mines." National Conservative leader Robert Borden, writing to Whitney on several other matters, added this paragraph: "The policy which you have laid down with regard to the mineral wealth of the province is a spendid departure from the traditions of the past. I commend it in every way and thoroughly congratulate you upon it. There appears to me no good reasons why great resources of this character should be handed over for the upbuilding of huge private fortunes instead of being reserved for the benefit of the whole community—for the establishment and maintenance of great educational institutions or otherwise for the benefit of the people at large."

The bill repealed all previous legislation on the subject except a few matters specifically stated. It provided, however, that any rights acquired, or any liabilities or penalties, under the previous legislation were not affected. Then it went on to state what was in effect a new bill of rights for the small prospector, giving him—or attempting to give him—the same rights as big companies.

For the first time there was a uniform law for the whole province which, in addition to giving protection to the prospector, provided for a decentralization of administration— moving administration to the mining areas themselves—and a security of titles which would provide protection for the investor.

The province would be divided into Mining Divisions and in each where sufficient business warranted it, a Mining Recorder's Office would be opened. On making a discovery of mineral, the prospector would stake out his claim by planting posts at the corners, and erect a discovery post on the outcrop. A claim would be a square of twenty chains (1320 feet) to a side; this amounting to 40 acres. The fee was $10 annually, with a restriction to three claims for any prospector in a year.

On staking his claim the prospector would record it in the office of the Mining Division. His discovery was subject to inspection. If the inspector found a discovery of valuable mineral, the prospector then would be required to do thirty days' work within ninety days of recording the claim, sixty days' work in each of the next two years, and ninety days' work during the third year. Or he could complete these days of work in a shorter time if he wished. He could then buy the land at

$3 per acre, if in surveyed territory, or $2.50 if in unsurveyed territory. This patent would be indefeasible (not forfeitable) and not subject to any further working conditions.

Under the bill, actual discovery of valuable mineral was necessary in order to obtain title to mining lands. Valuable mineral was defined in these words: "A vein, lode or other deposit of mineral or minerals in place, containing such quantities of mineral or minerals, other than limestone, marble, clay, marl, peat, or any building stone, as to make it probable that the said vein, lode or other deposit is capable of being developed into a working mine." This was an important guarantee against the blanketing technique—staking and recording lands simply because of their proximity to known mines or deposits of value.

In the main, mineral deposits of value in Ontario at that time outcropped at the surface; for this reason the law required actual discovery. There were, however, cases where owing to the depth of soil or upper covering of barren rock the minerals did not actually outcrop, and consequently were difficult or impossible to discover in the ordinary way. In such cases where it would be necessary to dig trenches, sink a shaft, or use a diamond drill, the bill permitted application to be made for what was called a Working Permit. This gave the holder exclusive possession of the claim for six months on condition of his working on it five days per week during that time. If at the end of six months he had not made a discovery, the permit could be renewed for another term. When discovery was made the land could be bought and patented in the ordinary way. This provision went a long way towards meeting views of some mining men who held that the Crown should not always insist upon visible discovery.

Prospecting permits were also provided for in the bill, mainly to cover substances such as petroleum, natural gas, salt, lignite, and other minerals that do not come to the surface in the ordinary way. A one-year Prospecting Permit covering 640 acres could be granted on payment of a fee of $100. The holder was required to spend in actual work a sum equal to $2 per acre. Upon the discovery of minerals the land could be leased subject to a rental of $1 per acre and the expenditure of $2 per acre per annum in raising the substances found.

The bill also regulated mining partnerships. It was common for two or more prospectors to work as partners, or a well-off man might grubstake a prospector. The bill required particulars of all partnerships to be filed in the Recorder's Office, with an agent to be named by the partnership with authority to deal with the claim. This would abolish silent partners.

The bill also placed miners and mine-labourers on the same level as mechanics, for legal and labour-law purposes.

Improved regulations were provided for the health and safety of working miners and detailed rules for the handling of explosives, ventilation, ladder-ways, shafts, scaling, etc.

At the same time, the Attorney General, J. J. Foy, introduced a measure to eliminate another contentious matter in the mining industry. Until then, mining companies could issue shares at a discount and without any personal liability—meaning that mining promoters were given a break not accorded to those in other businesses and industries. This exclusion of mining companies from the general law of the province was removed.

Another policy reflecting the new concern for public sharing in natural resources was announced about the same time by Premier Whitney. It concerned the potentially rich Gillies Limit. Premier Whitney said that the government was reserving, to be developed and mined for the benefit of the whole province, an area of three square miles adjoining the rich holdings at Cobalt. He also said that tenders would be considered for claims along three and a half miles of railway right-of-way in the region, considered to be prime property. But the lowest sum that would be accepted was $50,000 cash, a rental of $500 a year for building sites, and a royalty of from 10 per cent to 50 per cent on ore taken out.

The *Sudbury Journal,* while hailing the new bill as fair, enlightened, and long overdue, also noted that:

> A number of Sudburyites will be considerably disappointed at the price asked for the right-of-way, as we understand they had the promise of it on much easier conditions.
>
> In deciding to retain the rich section of the Gillies Limit, the Government is keeping an asset for the province which should bring in a good return for many years to come. Their decision also settles the question of its disposal in a manner which will probably give themselves less trouble than if disposed of in any other manner.

The *Globe* reported that, in moving second reading of his bill, "The Minister of Lands and Mines was clear and concise in his statement, and was heartily applauded by the government side." The Leader of the Opposition also stated his general approval. The subsequent debate during second reading and the committee stage was mild.

One question that brought some debate was whether, even if all the conditions of the Act were met, the government should grant non-forfeitable title. Shouldn't the province retain some right in those lands? Even by letting it out on perpetual lease? Frank Cochrane said he didn't think so; that it was impossible to encourage people to invest their money in mining properties if they didn't get something tangible, such as a land title, in return. Mining was a gamble. Large sums of money could be spent without a return. Would it be fair if men who spent that money should not have even possession of the land they were mining?

Other questions were asked about revenue to be derived from the mining industry by land taxes and royalties, but at one point Premier Whitney intervened to say that the honourable members should wait until the revenue provisions were brought down at the next session, and then argue if they wished.

Several essential matters apart from mining were proceeding at the same time in Cochrane's department. In the far north, a combined party of Ontario and Quebec surveyors were establishing for the first time the boundary line between the two provinces to within a few dozen miles of James Bay.

Also, for months Cochrane had been re-negotiating an old Liberal government contract with the Grand Trunk Pacific Railway for its Fort William branch line. Ontario originally had granted the Grand Trunk Pacific $2,000 a mile as a cash bonus, plus a whopping 1.2 million acres of land along the right-of-way. The company had agreed to place 400 settlers a year on the land. Probing the matter, Cochrane found this settlement part of the contract hadn't been fulfilled. He went to the Grand Trunk Pacific to ask why, and to state politely but firmly that as a result of this breach Ontario wanted some of the land back. The Grand Trunk Pacific countered with a land offer that Cochrane considered too low. The *Globe* reported: "Mr. Cochrane upheld his side of the case with considerable tact," and eventually the railway agreed to give up 525,000 acres of its grant. In announcing this to the press, Premier Whitney stated tersely: "The advantages to the Province are obvious."

Another widely accepted piece of Cochrane legislation in that session was the Veterans' Land Act, which had a remarkably simple and straightforward ring. Under the Act, certain townships would be set aside exclusively for veterans of Canadian military service as far back as the Fenian raids of 1866. Thousands of quarter-sections (160 acres each) were surveyed in Northern Ontario townships for this purpose. But if a veteran didn't wish to accept the free land, he could sell his rights to the government for $50 cash. The first $50,000 voted by the legislature under the Act was paid to veterans in the first six months after it became law, but other thousands of veterans took up land—440 in the Algoma district alone.

Even when legislatures are at their most peaceful, there are undercurrents. One of these in the 1906 session was an indirect reflection of Cochrane's flat "Pull is dead" a few months earlier. Many Conservative members felt that Pull should be resurrected immediately, if not sooner. People in their constituencies were looking for jobs as bailiffs, licence inspectors, and court clerks, and for other minor positions that could be opened immediately if the Liberal appointees now holding the jobs simply were fired—as had been the almost invariable custom in the past. These members became quite noisy in caucus and in public. One cabinet member said bluntly that Pull should be restored "to keep our friends in line. It is to them we have to look for aid and support. We can afford to lose the independents and the Liberals if we have to."

But Premier Whitney eventually got them all quietened down, with a silky statement that the government would regret losing the services and support of any colleague who could not heartily support its policy. If any member wished to supply evidence against an official and prove that he had been "offensively partisan" politically, that was different. But changes would not be made on straight party grounds alone.

The Liberals did score once in this argument, even after it had subsided. They asked how many officials in East and West Nipissing had been relieved of their duties and replaced with Conservatives since the election. The government replied that the total was 32 and gave the names. Among them were Crown lands agents, licence inspectors, constables, jailers, jail surgeons, fishery overseers, bailiffs, court clerks, issuers of marriage licences, forest and fire rangers, justices of the peace. One was the man loyal Charles Lamarche had replaced, John Loughrin, who was a registrar, master of titles, and police magistrate.

When the legislature rose that spring, Cochrane began a custom that was to occupy every summer, and some winters, from then on: touring the North with as many influential guests as he could persuade to come along. Late in May he took a legislative group, and newsmen, along the full length of the

Temiskaming and Northern Ontario Railway to the end of
steel about 300 miles north of Toronto and still 150 miles short
of James Bay. After a couple of weeks in his office he set off
again, this time for ten days in the Thunder Bay and Rainy
River districts, seeking, said the *Globe*, "personal knowledge of
questions relative to the interests of settlers and miners in the
districts, with which his department had constantly to deal."
He visited Port Arthur, Fort William, Wabigoon, Denoric,
Dryden, Kenora, Rainy River, Fort Frances, and Sturgeon
Falls, and gave a glowing account to Toronto interviewers of
what he had found: a need for roads and drainage, but a good
potential for fine agricultural development. Two months later
he announced that the province soon would establish an
agricultural experimental station in the North to carry this
program along. He was in the North again in September with
a few other ministers. Back in Toronto he told a luncheon
audience that his department had the highest revenue of any
in the government, and that 95 to 97 per cent of it came from
Northern Ontario. So the rest of Ontario had to be prepared to
spend money to help the North develop even more. He was
acting like a two-way missionary, selling the North both to the
south and to northerners themselves.

An echo of Cochrane's old battlegrounds was heard again
about that time. His opposition to an export duty on nickel
matte eight years before, as mayor of Sudbury, had been based
on his conviction—disputed hotly by others—that such a tax
would hurt Canada's nickel in the world market and not
achieve the aim of encouraging Canadian refineries. Before his
first legislative session he said in a speech that he hoped to
introduce legislation to encourage the refining in Ontario of all
nickel mined in the province. That turned out eventually to be
legislation that was put over until 1907. But he had made the
promise that government support was on the way. And late in
the year he travelled north to the Cobalt region to the first
smelting and refining plant ever erected by Canadians for the
treatment of Canadian ores. A special train from North Bay

carried guests to this ceremony. Flanked by area members of both the House of Commons and the provincial legislature, Cochrane laid the cornerstone after listening to a large number of speeches paying tribute to him and to the Ontario government for providing aid and encouragement in making possible the custom refining of silver, cobalt, and nickel from area mines. Previously, all these ores had to be shipped in matte form to smelters and refineries in the United States, lessening Canadian participation in the full value of Canadian ore. There is no mistaking the connection between that enthusiasm for an all-Canadian refinery and smelter in 1906 and the same enthusiasm more than six decades later for anything that makes the fullest use in terms of employment and profits—in Canada! —of Canadian natural resources.

CHAPTER FIVE

Early in 1907 there were some wry happenings in the Toronto press that had their private repercussions at the Cochrane home on Maple Avenue. Alice Cochrane was a strong-minded woman, and although she occasionally now entertained at home for small groups of members and their wives, and was entertained at the home of the Lieutenant-Governor on state occasions (such as the visit of Prince Arthur, the Duke of Connaught, to Toronto), she had never lost her distaste for her husband's involvement in politics. Her children, growing up, were aware of this as being occasionally the subject of family arguments. More than once these had ended only with the closing of the front door as Frank Cochrane took off hastily for his office.

Partly, Alice Cochrane's objections to his heavy work load had to do with his health. The loss of his leg at the age of fifty-two had been more of a blow than he had publicly admitted; and this was aggravated by the pace he set himself. She had extracted one promise from him late in 1906—that they would take a holiday in Europe as soon as his second-stage mining bills were passed in the 1907 session. When the word got out, there was speculation that Cochrane's health had become so bad that he was preparing to resign. Cochrane denied this emphatically, saying he was in excellent health. Premier Whitney said he had "heard nothing and desired to hear nothing."

Through it all, the family got the impression that Mrs. Cochrane simply thought her husband would be better employed, and their lives happier and more private, if he took a more relaxed course through life, allowing them both to enjoy the fair-sized income that had accrued through his previous business, mining, and timber interests, as well as the slowly growing power company at Wahnapitae. She had been especially offended in 1905 when every newspaper, for a while, seemed to be trying to outdo every other newspaper in sarcasm and doubt about her husband's appointment to the cabinet. This "bad press" may have affected her husband's lifetime outlook on the press, as well; especially when one considers his early experience in Sudbury with the pesky editor of the *Journal*. At any rate, there is no evidence anywhere that Cochrane ever had a crony or even a confidant in the press, as many politicians then and since have had, to ensure that in contentious matters they have at least one friendly access to print.

But tides do turn. There had been some open admiration in the smaller provincial weeklies and dailies in 1906, along with an apparent armistice on the matter in the Toronto press. But when the session of 1907 opened with Cochrane's three new bills on mining dominating political debate, the press turn-around was complete. For instance, the *Toronto News* was a politically independent newspaper. Its editor was John Willison —once editor of the arch-Liberal *Globe*. Although Joseph Flavelle, owner of the *News*, was a Tory, his relationship with Whitney had often been acerbic, as was Willison's on occasion. In 1905 Flavelle had told Whitney that some actions of his government were "so completely at variance with Mr. Willison's and my own views as to what is in the public interest, that the News will be outspoken and insistent in its condemnation of this or similar acts of your government." In short, the *News* was not a slavish government supporter.

Yet on February 25, 1907, Willison's editorial in the *News* about the new Tory mining legislation was headed "A Bold Minister", and continued:

> It is very probable that Mr. Frank Cochrane, Minister of Lands, Forests and Mines, will find his new mining bill will seriously affect his political standings in Northern Ontario. He represents the constituency in which Cobalt is situated. This is a mining community. In fact 95 percent of the mining men of the Province regard Mr. Cochrane as their representative in the Legislature. Yet ... he has brought down a bill which excites the hostility of all mining men. If Mr. Cochrane were a practical politician he would have hesitated before putting his seat in apparent jeopardy. But he is a business man. He is convinced that the interest of the Province demands just such a bill as he has introduced, and he is bold enough to give practical effect to his convictions in spite of the opinions of many of his constituents. When the interests of his electors and the interests of the Province clashed, Mr. Cochrane took the side of the Province. This is a refreshing change from the spirit of county politics so often seen not only in Queen's Park, but on Parliament Hill.

Elsewhere in the same issue of the *News*, another article hailed the bill as "recognition of the rights of the people of the province to benefit in some degree from the rich mineral stores of the North", and noted that Cochrane's "intentions generally are carried out, if thought and energy can accomplish it."

The *Globe* chimed in with an editorial hailing one part of the Mining Revenue Bill debate as showing the legislature

> at its best as a parliamentary chamber in action. The subject under discussion was exceptionally difficult, bristling with details and affording little in the way of experience to guide lawmakers through its mazes. The Minister of Lands and Mines was responsible for the

bill under discussion, and he displayed a good deal of tact and skill in piloting it through committee . . .

The *Ottawa Citizen*'s glowing comment was to the effect that

> The Hon. Mr. Cochrane is evidently of the fibre that statesmen are made of. . . . He courageously persevered in the face of all local influence [in the North] that could be brought to bear upon him by men who were his personal friends and most staunch political adherents. At the same time he acted with such tact and fairness as won him the respect of even those who took a contrary view. Such instances of faithful adherence to principle under pressure of conflicting interests, where the duty of a minister to the people at large comes into opposition with the claims of a constituency on its member, are sufficiently rare to merit special commendation. It stamps Hon. Mr. Cochrane as one of the most valuable men we have in public life.

The *North Bay Tribune,* in the heart of the country most opposed to anything that might cut into mining profits, checked in with the word that Mr. Cochrane

> conducts his department in a manner which must command admiration even from those who do not see eye to eye with him. . . . Mr. Cochrane refuses to deviate from his convictions . . .

The *Canadian Courier* called his rise "meteoric" and in a general survey of his political career said that

> Since entering upon his duties, Mr. Cochrane has become known as a hard worker and careful administrator, who pays more than ordinary personal attention to the details of his department. He is prompt to act, and follows pretty rigidly what he conceives to be his proper course at any time, which explains why he is sometimes bitterly assailed by those who do not agree with him.

Some people also would like the rather acid comment of the *Toronto Star,* that imposing a royalty on mines merely touched the fringe of the question.

> What Mr. Cochrane should get at is the [mining]
> prospectuses [through which mining stocks were sold].
> A flat rate of $10 per adjective would bring in an
> enormous revenue to the province.

It is doubtful that any of this praise permanently changed
Alice Cochrane's feeling about her husband's being in politics.
But she was never again able to claim that her husband was
not appreciated, probably for some of the same qualities of
adamancy and non-deviation that from time to time prolonged
their occasional differences of opinion at home in Rosedale.
And for the first time that winter she exercised the preroga-
tive of the wife of a senior cabinet minister and entertained
at Queen's Park. The *News* reported that her reception and
tea was so largely attended that it overflowed the dining
room into the members' luncheon room, with "a bevy of
girls in dainty light frocks including Miss Cochrane in pink
mousseline and lace; Miss Whitney in white lace; and Miss
Bethune in black with a white transparent yoke" mingling
with major Ontario political figures of the day and their
wives. Mrs. Cochrane wore ivory Spanish lace and had the
room set with Roman hyacinths, white jonquils, carnations,
and azaleas to distract the mind from the messy winter
outside. Her sister, Miss Dunlap from Pembroke, assisted—
and over there was the globular figure of Premier Whitney,
the ramrod limp of Silent Frank, and the affable and ever-
popular (among voters, if not in cabinet) Adam Beck, and
many other prominent Liberals and Tories, chaffing one
another as politicians often do when temporarily out of the
trenches. It was the sort of scene that could be repeated among
the womenfolk of any legislature today, except that probably
today there would be something stronger than tea.

One can only wonder whether this reception was planned
before or after the mingled anguish and praise sounded in
response to news of the large needle that Frank Cochrane was
about to jab into the well-upholstered mining industry with
his three new mining bills. He didn't present them to the

legislature until February 13, but their general contents were known widely enough to cause hot debate well in advance. When the legislature met on Tuesday, January 29, new Liberal leader George P. Graham, a lively newspaperman from Brockville, demanded some answers from Premier Whitney with regard to mining legislation, and was treated to an urbane put-off, followed by the statement that the government was fortunate in having Mr. Cochrane to handle these matters —"a man of the highest character, equal in capacity of any man who ever sat on the treasury benches of the legislature".

Eleven days later, with the legislation still not public, Cochrane took up an entire Saturday morning meeting a delegation of big-wheel lawyers and accountants representing mining interests. They complained in advance about the possibility of acreage taxation, especially on lands that were not being worked, and made a wide variety of laments. On the matter of lands that weren't being worked, although held as mines, Cochrane gave the cheerful opinion that a land tax would be an impetus to the land-holders to get to work and find out if the properties were worth mining or should be turned back to agricultural or forestry purposes.

To this deputation he repeated his earlier promise of what was to become one of his strongest arguing points in later debate: that revenue to be derived from new taxes would be used to support and encourage the refining and smelting of ores in this province. He felt "that the government would be doing something greatly in the interests of mining men if they could bring about such a condition. It did not seem right that Ontario ores should be shipped from Canada to another country for treatment. [The other country, of course, was mainly the United States.] The place for refining and smelting was right here."

After this meeting, Cochrane went directly to a Saturday afternoon cabinet meeting, after which Premier Whitney assured newspapermen, in answer to questions, that the new mining bills would be brought in the following week; then they would all know what was being talked about.

Cochrane introduced the three bills to the legislature for first reading on the following Wednesday. One, as the mining interests had feared, provided for taxation not only on mining acreage but on annual profits—a full 3 per cent on annual net profits with the first $10,000 exempt! (Many companies would not mind that kind of "crippling" impost today.)

The second bill set out terms for the encouragement of refining and smelting in the province by paying bounties up to six cents a pound for refined metallic nickel, oxide of nickel, metallic cobalt, and oxide of cobalt, with lesser payments for metallic copper, sulphate of copper, and white arsenic. Maximum bounties were set so that in all categories a refinery could not collect from the government more than $60,000 a year for nickel, the same for copper, $30,000 for cobalt, and $15,000 for arsenic. To qualify for any bounty a refinery had to be ready and willing at all times to smelt, heat, and refine ores of all comers, or buy the ores for later treatment at going market rates. This provision obviously would open the refineries and smelters to small operators as well as large. (It took the passage of years to show that this encouragement, while well meant, was not high enough to draw a major nickel refinery into the province.)

The third bill was a hodge-podge of amendments to the Mines Act of 1906; the sort of legislation that is known today as housekeeping—clarifying several points that had proved to be unclear in the original.

When debate began on second reading of the bills, February 21, it was obvious that apart from some minor nit-picking, and some well-taken arguments on the matter of taxing natural gas, the legislative opposition wasn't going to be too tough. C. N. Smith, the member for Sault Ste. Marie, thought (and turned out to be right) that the bonuses for refining and smelt-

The Honourable Frank
Cochrane (*Public Archives
of Canada*)

Alice Dunlap Cochrane

ABOVE Robert Borden, Edmund Bristol, Frank Cochrane, Dr. J. O. Réaume, and Sir James Whitney discuss the strategy that would result in a Conservative sweep of Ontario in the federal election of 1911. (*Public Archives of Canada*)

BELOW The Conservative convention in South Porcupine, June 13, 1914.

RIGHT At the site of the Coquitlam (B.C.) water supply dam in July 1912. Seated are J. D. Taylor, M.P., F. McKenzie, M.L.A., Mr. Cochrane, H. H. Stevens, M.P., and F. R. Glover.

BELOW A cruise along the North Saskatchewan River during the visit to Prince Albert in July 1912. Mr. Cochrane is seated just above the 'G' in *George V*.

GEORGE V

UPPER LEFT   Mr. Cochrane with a group of officials outside the Welland Ship Canal office in July 1914.

LOWER LEFT   Mr. Cochrane and party stop for luncheon along the shore of the Nelson River on the way to Hudson Bay, August 1912.

BELOW   Mr. Cochrane with Premier J. A. Mathieson of Prince Edward Island and General Superintendent Brady, 1912.

On the trip north, according to George W. Yates, Mr. Cochrane paddled every foot of the way.

ABOVE Mr. Cochrane with Captain Dalton of the *Stanley*, viewing icebergs during the return voyage from the inspection of the projected route of the Hudson Bay Railway, September 1912.

BELOW The Cochrane party with the Captain on the afterdeck of the *Stanley*.

ing would be better if they were bigger, and paid in lump sums rather than by the pound, but after that he subsided.

The real opposition was outside the legislature, from the mining industry itself against the new taxes on its revenue. The heat thus generated flowed strongly towards Queen's Park. Mining men sought out their local members and told them to get on the ball, get in there and fight, or there wouldn't be any generous campaign funds forthcoming in the next election. At a meeting in Cobalt, mining men and mine managers were said by the *Globe* to be "up in arms" as they passed "a strongly-worded resolution" directed to Cochrane and giving reasons for their displeasure. They said they would load a deputation into a special train and go to Toronto to protest in person, as soon as they could obtain an interview. They added up all the taxes already being paid by the industry and claimed that any more would discourage the investment of needed capital. (Some things haven't changed in sixty-five years.) They also wanted a royal commission to investigate the whole matter.

Some reverse heat or back-firing was immediately evident in political circles. On the day that the outspoken demands of the big Cobalters were published in Toronto, the member for Dufferin, Dr. F. D. Lewis, told a North Toronto political meeting that if the mining men in Cobalt carried out their threats to unseat Frank Cochrane, he (Dr. Lewis) would resign and offer his seat to the mines minister. No greater loyalty hath any politician.

But the press and the public continued to supply ample muscle in Cochrane's support. The Tory *Mail and Empire* sniffed that the opposition had been expected, because

> it would be hypocrisy for any man, no matter how public-spirited he might be, to pretend to be wholly pleased with legislation to increase his contribution to the public treasury. . . . The broad, human antipathy to taxes is probably all that is behind the resolution that some of the Cobalt mining interests have passed

> in condemnation of the bill. . . . The producing mines
> of the Cobalt region ... are among the richest in the
> world; they have until recently been the property of
> the public, and the public have received next to nothing
> for them. They should be taxed, and not sparingly
> taxed.

The big Cobalters made good their threat of an invasion of Toronto by special train. They arrived at the King Edward Hotel en masse on a Thursday night and held a hot meeting to plan their strategy for the following day. They then proceeded, some on foot and some by carriage or motor car, to Queen's Park in such numbers that they filled the largest reception room. There they were joined by several representatives of Toronto stock brokers, and faced Premier Whitney and his mines minister.

The temper of the meeting was set early by Frank Cochrane. Most of these men were his friends or acquaintances, but he said bluntly they had known ever since the previous September that these bills were on the way. The matter also had been mentioned in the Speech from the Throne in January. He thought it unfair for them to protest at this late hour.

The first speaker for the delegation was a Toronto man, W. Boultbee, saying that a protest had been sent by the Coniagas mine, which he represented. Here Cochrane's encyclopedic knowledge of his subject showed sharply. "That particular mine should be the last to kick," he informed Mr. Boultbee coldly. "They have an asset worth between three and four million dollars, and all the government ever got out of it was a simple fee of a hundred and twenty dollars."

He went on to say that railways and other corporations paid taxes and that the Canadian Copper Company at Sudbury, largest mining corporation in the province, already had agreed to pay any fair tax. As points were raised by the delegation, Cochrane steadfastly, but politely, knocked them down—assisted occasionally by Premier Whitney. The whole hysterical nature of mining booms was discussed, and Cochrane chided persons who encouraged such boom psychology, adding, perhaps with a little irony, that his remarks did not apply to those present, most of whom he knew to be genuinely interested in practical mining, rather than pushing mining stocks. As charges and counter-charges flew from one subject to another, Cochrane noted aloud that the delegation was united on one point, anyway—opposition to the tax.

In both the *Globe* and the *News,* reports on this confrontation ran to almost 2,000 words, or two columns of type. In the *Globe,* as well, a 500-word editorial cautioned that mining royalties and taxes should not be levied in a way that would injure the industry, but reasserted the right of the public to share in mineral wealth discovered on public property. The *News*' headline covered the matter in a nutshell: "Mining Tax Stays—Mr. Cochrane's Reply to Big Delegation".

But a week later when Cochrane moved second reading of the bill, he said he had given ground on one point. His personal view, as he had told the Cobalt delegation, was that the tax on mine profits should be on a sliding scale upward— with the richest companies paying the highest rates of tax. He now told the House that this feature had proved objectionable to the mining men, "and their arguments were convincing enough to lead to a change from the sliding scale to a uniform rate." The effect would be, he said, that the man or company who was careful and economical, and therefore achieved higher profits, would not be penalized by a higher tax rate.

It became obvious during this stage of the debate, and later in the clause-by-clause committee stage, that when the bills came to a vote there would not be a split on straight party lines. Some Liberals stated their support for the bills, and one went so far (reported the *News*) as to congratulate the minister for having dealt capably and well with a difficult problem. When there was opposition, Cochrane was equal to it. After one criticism had been made that the tax would militate against the industry generally, he countered with a few words about the Nipissing Mine. "It was public land," he said, "bought at $3 an acre, sold for $200,000, later capitalized at $6,000,000, and now said to be worth $33,000,000. It is therefore felt that the public should receive something more from such valuable lands." The bill would achieve this end by taxing net profits, as well as acreage.

One area with which he was not so familiar was natural gas, a matter of great concern to members from those southwestern Ontario communities that used it most. Many householders used their own gas wells for home consumption, and in others the gas supply was a community affair. Some gas was exported, mainly in the Niagara region where U.S. money had been used for development of gas wells and the owners decided to bring gas back across the border as part of their return on their investment. Cochrane laid some fears to rest by saying that the tax was not intended for persons using their own supplies, but only when the gas was sold on a commercial basis. A few days later this was spelled out. The gas would be taxed at two cents per thousand feet, but there would be a 90 per cent tax rebate for all gas used for domestic purposes (meaning, in Canada). In effect, therefore, this constituted a form of export tax in the only way a province could manage such a thing—simply by making gas not used in Canada not subject to the 90 per cent tax rebate. Householders using their own gas wells would pay no tax at all, as before.

The visit of a large delegation protesting the gas tax said flatly, and rather threateningly, that although they supported the mining tax and were supporters of the government, this new gas tax would drastically reduce Conservative votes in the districts affected. This prompted another Cochrane statement that was hailed in the press. "I had hoped that the day was past when the argument of vote-getting or vote-losing was supposed to weigh with a minister over what he believed to be right, and in the interests of the province," he said.

"Up in the north, in my own constituency, among my own people engaged and interested in the mining operations, they do not feel kindly to the mining tax, which you endorse. I don't think it is a vote-getter for me. I know it isn't. It is because I think it right in the interests of the whole Province that I submit it to the Legislature. It may not be politics. I don't suppose it is. But will we be any the worse for trying principle, instead of politics, for a while?"

There was more than a slight aura of haste about the final stages of the mining bills. When the Canadian Mining Institute met in Toronto, among the items on its agenda were a banquet, attended by Cochrane and other government ministers; and a meeting with Cochrane at Queen's Park. At this meeting, which could have developed into another protracted debate, Cochrane asserted again that his mining bills were going through and would be law within a few days. But if the Mining Institute wished to take the legislation, redraft it, and submit the draft within a year, he would consider the suggested changes in his housekeeping legislation on the bills later. This sent them away mollified, pledging that they would draft such a new bill, and stating the personal confidence that they had in Frank Cochrane. Four days later the mining bills cleared the committee stage and therefore were ready for the perfunctory third reading, and clear passage. Another three days later, Frank Cochrane and his wife sailed for Europe.

He might not have realized it then, but the bills just passed —while they would be refined almost year by year in future— would stand as his most important legislative contribution to Ontario.

CHAPTER SIX

No one in Canadian public life today encounters anything approaching the sheer fury of an election such as the one held in Ontario in 1908. Cochrane had been plunged—apparently enjoying every minute of it—into one of the most critical periods in a half-century of Ontario politics. The Ontario Liberals had been in power so long (and Liberals were in power in Ottawa, under Laurier, and in Quebec, under Gouin) that they felt 1905 was a temporary aberration. Given another chance, they were sure Ontario voters would come to their senses and throw the Tories out. In mid 1907 the Conservatives professed to have no fears on that score, but still went about preparing for the following year's election like a prudent general preparing for an attack.

A remarkable amount of the sheer work involved fell to Frank Cochrane. A reading of newspapers in the period demonstrates that no other minister covered as much ground, talked in as many smoky back rooms, sat on as many platforms. His own situation was a matter of public discussion. When the *Hamilton Herald* published in July 1907 an assessment of what would happen in Toronto in the yet-unannounced election, Cochrane was listed as a likely candidate in North Toronto—although, the *Herald* said,

> Much depends. . . . The Minister of lands and mines
> has thus far consistently refused to countenance any
> suggestion that he run for a Toronto seat. The sugges-
> tion, however, is made in good faith and is an apprecia-
> tion of . . . his courage and fairness in placing the
> interests of the province before those of his [northern]
> constituency.

Obviously some Conservatives were beginning to worry that
his firmness in dealing with the mining interests might back-
fire against him in the North. They wanted him to run where
he would be safe.

Cochrane seemed as robust as ever, even though the 1907
holiday in Europe had been cut short. He and his wife had
been away only a short time when their son Ogden, left at
home, contracted typhoid fever. The Cochranes weren't told,
because the case was not serious, but then Edith Dunlap, Mrs.
Cochrane's sister, also became ill, and gravely so. The
Cochranes, cabled in Rome, headed for home immediately
but Miss Dunlap died before they arrived early in May.
With Ogden nearly fully recovered, the family headed north
on Dominion Day. Cochrane dropped his family for the
summer at Haileybury on Lake Temiskaming and travelled
west to the Lakehead with a group of northern members and
ministers. He was back in the eastern part of the North a few
weeks later on a special train bearing members of the American Institute of Mining Engineers, acting as their host—and
using every public occasion along the way for politicking.
He obviously realized that because of the unpopularity of the
mining bills in the North, the party's fate as well as his own
was involved. To many in that vast area of scattered population from Fort Frances in the west to Pembroke in the
east, he *was* the Conservative party. As he went, so other
northern candidates would go. Accordingly, the summer and
autumn of 1907 shaped up as one long pre-election trip.
Noting this, newspapers in the North took largely predictable
sides. The *North Bay Tribune* reported in July that the visit

of Frank Cochrane and Agriculture Minister Nelson Mon-
teith to Temiskaming

> resolved itself into a succession of hearty welcomes,
> which demonstrated beyond question that any dis-
> affection that may have existed had been consigned
> to an early, a permanent and a very deep tomb. . . . The
> greater part was the work of foreign boomsters who
> were only living for the present, who cared nothing for
> future development.

But the *Silver City News,* in Cobalt, saw it differently in
September, reporting that Cochrane

> . . . while in town recently, was advised to quietly fade
> from view politically before the next election takes
> place. The advice was given by a Cochrane political
> admirer, who wanted to do his bosom friend an ever-
> lasting favor and save him from possible defeat. . . . No
> man could get the vote of the ore belt in the next
> election who has no better policy to offer than what we
> are getting at present.

The *Temiskaming Herald* fired back in October that this
display of claws from the *Silver City News* mainly reflected
the fact that Cyril T. Young, owner of the *News,* was going to
run for the Liberal nomination.

> The News is following the established practice of the
> tied journal, whose allegiance is first to party and then
> to truth.

In Cochrane's fence-mending and fence-assessing through
the North that autumn, he didn't miss many stops. During a
typical two days in mid October, between leaving the Thursday night train from Toronto and boarding the southbound
for the return journey Saturday night, he visited the small
communities of Hillview, Tomstown, Hilliardton, Judges, and
St. Antoine, holding large meetings and listening to all comers,
most of them seeking better roads and more bridges. He left
in his wake a fairly sure undercurrent that was expressed by
the *Temiskaming Herald* in a way that was becoming preva-

lent: a tendency to contrast his manner favourably with that
of more garrulous politicians of the time.

> Mr. Cochrane is not a speechmaker. That is he does
> not play in literary fireworks and froth, to that ante-
> diluvian bitterness called grit or tory when discussing
> public affairs, but he does tell a straightforward story.
> Cochrane is not an orator. Well perhaps not. He does
> not dance a cakewalk to the tune of an idea, nor yet work
> up a scene in heavy tragedy in giving birth to a sentence.
> He does not make an all-fired fuss about handing out
> a few passing thoughts but he does make an interesting
> speech, full of facts and grey matter. His tone of mind
> is frank, fair and moderate. His delivery is easy and
> fluent and his bearing manly and businesslike. All that
> may not be oratory, but it is good speaking that
> counts for infinitely more than political lather.

At the same time, he continuously refused to make con-
ciliatory concessions in the area where he was said to be
vulnerable. When Larder Lake prospectors pleaded that the
plague of flies and the absence of roads should persuade the
government to give them more time to explore their claims, he
grudgingly gave them a few more weeks—but then fought
brusquely and publicly against a longer extension that was
handed out by Whitney through an order-in-council. The
cabinet obviously believed he needed any help he could
get.

Even the *Globe*, which was to lead a baying anti-Conservative pack within a few months, carried late that year a
picture of Cochrane leaving Queen's Park with Public Works
Minister Réaume after a cabinet meeting. The underline noted
(in words the *Globe* editor possibly wished he could recall,
later),

> Mr. Cochrane has proved himself an indefatigable
> worker and possessed of initiative in regard to methods
> by which crown lands may be made to add to the public
> funds. He has attained a reputation even in dealing
> with political friends, of straightforward bluntness. Be-

hind his brusque manner is a kindly and likeable temperament.

Only a few months later the *Globe* was carrying almost daily editorials castigating Cochrane, along with all other members of the Whitney government—but by then the election was closer and the campaign was really on in earnest.

It was a dirty campaign. While most of the partisan polemics were fired at Premier Whitney, dead aim was taken at Cochrane with a succession of charges trying to link him with political skulduggery of one kind or another, as if bringing down the government's most right-seeming man would also seriously injure the party as a whole.

Two of these cases, one of which got to court, involved the methods by which Cochrane had obtained his acclamation in 1905. Why the principals had waited until another election was in the offing before taking action seems fairly plain: part of the mud-slinging election tactics of the time.

On January 13, 1908, an engineer named Henry Draney filed a statement of claim in his suit for $130,000 damages against Frank B. Chapin, miner, of Toronto; George T. Smith, Mining Recorder, Haileybury; Charles Lamarche, Master of Titles for Nipissing; and C. A. Masten, barrister, Toronto.

Draney claimed that about May 5, 1905, he had made an ore discovery at the bottom of Cobalt Lake, but when he applied to register the claim he had been turned down by Recorder Smith. On appealing to Thomas Gibson, Deputy Minister of Mines in Toronto, that ruling had been upheld. But two days later, Draney claimed, he had been approached by Chapin who said that in return for a half-interest in the claim he could use influence at Queen's Park to have the claim approved. On May 15, Draney claimed, he had been approached again by Chapin and Lamarche (who at that time was still the member for East Nipissing). Chapin said, Draney swore, that the government had agreed to grant the claim— but only if Lamarche would resign his seat in favour of

Frank Cochrane! Lamarche, said Draney, agreed to do this if Draney would give him a one-sixth interest in the claim.

On May 30, Cochrane was sworn in as mines minister. Lamarche promptly resigned his seat. Recorder Smith recorded the claim, representing, Draney said, that his orders to do so came directly from Cochrane. Cochrane duly was returned by acclamation to the seat Lamarche had vacated. On July 26, 1905, Draney conveyed to H. S. Strathy, general manager of the Traders Bank, all his interests in the claim with instructions to split the eventual proceeds on the basis of 8/27 each to Draney, Chapin, and Lamarche, and 3/27 to a partner named Milo Bessey who had actually recorded the claim. On July 29, Recorder Smith issued a recording receipt to Strathy. But then on August 14 the whole complicated apparatus blew up when the government, by order-in-council (certainly instigated by Cochrane), withdrew Cobalt Lake from sale, lease, or location. Still, Draney sold his part interest for $135,000. But on December 21, 1906, the government sold the whole property by public tender to a Cobalt syndicate for $1,085,000, wiping out Draney's deal as well as everybody else's. This matter was indirectly the subject of still another legal action at the time in which the Florence Lake Mining Company also said it had prior rights to Cobalt Lake, on a discovery made by William James Green early in 1906— which Recorder Smith had refused to register. Frank Cochrane testified in that suit, although refusing to answer certain questions on the grounds that they would force him to reveal cabinet secrets. He was upheld in this refusal by Mr. Justice Riddell, hearing the case.

In the end, the government's refusal to grant the claims to Draney and Green was upheld, and the Cobalt syndicate was confirmed as the purchaser. This case was one of many disputed claims rising from rapid policy changes as the government tried to control the summer boom of 1905. It seems possible that Charles Lamarche's intention to resign in favour of Cochrane, which had been known to a few before Draney's original discovery, might have been used retroactively by certain sharpies who knew he was going to resign, and saw a way to use what was a *fait accompli* in conning part of Draney's rights away from him. The government was said to have known the facts for some time before Draney's court action was taken. One possibility is that when the circumstances were made known to the government, in mid 1905, it accelerated action to withdraw the whole lake from anyone's claim. (It was on related points that Cochrane refused to testify.) The later sale by public tender was a policy that Cochrane had enunciated in the first weeks of his ministry, as a means by which the sale of public lands or mineral rights could benefit the public purse rather than so richly line those of mining entrepreneurs. It would have been in keeping with political practice of that time (or this, for that matter) to try to protect Lamarche—if he indeed had a knowing part in the fleecing of Draney. When Mr. Justice Riddell upheld Frank Cochrane's right to refuse answers to certain questions, this protecting of Lamarche (if such it was) was made possible.

But this case, cloaked in an impenetrable maze of conflicting claims, didn't play as large a part in the election as two others that were laid at Cochrane's door. These did not come along until the election campaign was formally under way—although the distinction between formal and informal electioneering was difficult to find. For instance, given the fact that the 1908 winter session of the legislature was imminent, and that travel in the North in January was a matter of huge fur coats and buffalo lap robes, and of horses pulling loaded sleighs from hotels or railway stations to meeting-halls through temperatures more often than not below zero, still Frank Cochrane spent much of the winter in the North. He was in North Bay in his home constituency of East Nipissing just after New Year's for a reception and banquet in his honour; 70 were invited, the *North Bay Tribune* reported, but 150 came—"party ties were forgotten and all united in the endeavour to do honour to the distinguished representative of East Nipissing."

Cochrane was back in North Bay a couple of weeks later to speak at the nomination meeting of his old friend George Gordon, who would contest the House of Commons seat there in the federal election to be held later in the year. It was federal business—but Conservatives were Conservatives, and it was a chance to pep them up for the provincial campaign as well. The *Sudbury Mining News* reported that while there was a big ovation for George Gordon, when Frank Cochrane got up to speak,

> the applause was beyond all description. He was look-ing his best, his face was wreathed in smiles, he was in the midst of warm friends. No matter where his eye rested he saw veterans who had sat with him at con-vention after convention, who had fought the fight when friends were few and opponents numerous.

In February, with the new session of the legislature, one of the first of the new bills was aimed directly at the North. In Cochrane's travels he had found dissatisfaction among settlers who homesteaded land and then found that they only owned surface rights. His bill, an amendment to the Public Lands Act, he said was designed to give effect to the government's new policy of "everything for the settler". There had been some difficulty in the North, he said, when settlers tried to farm land that was not suited to agricultural purposes. In future, government experts would decide what land was best for agriculture and then, when it was opened for settlement, the settlers would also receive mineral rights. This drew some Opposition sneers that the government first would ascertain that no minerals were present on the land, and then would bestow upon the settlers rights to the minerals that weren't there. But generally it was well received—especially when Cochrane followed quickly with plans to revise existing timber practices. Where timber lands were found to be good for agricultural purposes, the timber barons would be given only a limited time to get the timber off, instead of holding large timber limits for many years and thereby preventing settlers from getting on the land. Some such limits still held in 1908 had been granted before 1892. There would be new regulations governing timber-cutting, too, with only mature timber to be cut, and reforestation to take place in all parts of the province. In older Ontario tracts of land that were poor for farming would be replanted and returned to forest.

Even while the legislature was in session, there were few Conservative election meetings that Cochrane did not attend. The *Northern Advance*, at Barrie, covered a meeting at the Grand Opera House that had Conservatives from both the federal and the provincial fields present. One local politician, Billy Bennett, was described enthusiastically, if rather grue-somely, as a man feared by his opponents, and no wonder,

> He crams the umbrella down their throats and then opens it out.

Cochrane followed, stating that the Whitney government might have made mistakes but there had been no graft. Said the *Northern Advance*:

> There are no frills about Mr. Cochrane. Just plain, straightforward talk.

He was in Emsdale a few days later for the Parry Sound nominations and, reported the *Sundridge Echo,* supported the nomination of John Galna, the sitting member, and

> showed that grants to roads and schools in the Parry Sound area had been increased and [noted that] timberlands were now being put on sale in smaller parcels, giving the man with small capital a chance to invest.

In a meeting in East Toronto, supporting the federal can-didacy of A. E. Kemp, M.P., he and Education Minister R. A. Pyne were among the speakers. This time Cochrane touched the familiar ground of other meetings, but also noted that his new Mining Act was a great improvement over the old one because it had taken the administration of mining claims out of politics, with appeals being heard not by the minister (as had been the case when he first entered the legislature) but by the courts.

Meanwhile, with all this political activity, he kept a wary eye on other northern undercurrents—including a meeting of about 600 persons in Sturgeon Falls who urged that Northern Ontario should secede and run its own affairs as a separate province. Cochrane was the most common whipping-boy at this meeting for, one speaker said, "his tendency to destroy vested rights and override old legislative undertaking". But there was a bit of comedy in that. The secession motion at first was declared defeated, and was so reported in the *Sudbury Mining News* and the *Toronto News*. Then others who had been present came forward with affidavits declaring that the secession motion had indeed been carried. A Dr. Howey of Sudbury, an anti-secessionist, created a further furor by a public statement that

> I am not worrying, but am only looking for a govern-ment job. For if the silly, ridiculous and nonsensical speeches of these secessionist agitators ever reach To-ronto, we shall likely see in the supplementary estimates a large appropriation for a mammoth lunatic asylum in New Ontario. I am desirous of demonstrating to the government that I am sufficiently sane to be eligible to be appointed to the lucrative position of medical superintendent of that institution.

That one kept the editor of the *Sudbury Journal,* and his letters-to-the-editor writers, in a busy froth for several weeks.

No election date had been set by the time the legislature prorogued on April 14. But the *Globe*'s front-page headline on the day before the sessions ended stated: "Either June or September to be Time of Elections". And followed this with an editorial-page note, heavy with irony,

> The Ontario elections are to be held before or after June 15. This candor on the part of Whitney he parades

in contrast with the secrecy of other governments regarding such matters.

A word here about the *Globe*. During most of the Whitney term of office, this traditionally Liberal newspaper had acted more like an independent, giving the government a fair hearing and some support. In fact, Whitney had stated on one platform that he would be quite content to use the *Globe*'s editorial pages as his election manifesto. But about this time the *Globe* made a complete turnabout, and hammered away day after day at the record of the government. Whitney explained this caustically from another platform. The parade of grafters and cheats and hangers-on of the Liberal party that had been going up the stairs of the *Globe* lately, he said, had forced the editor to alter drastically his previously fair-minded attitude.

The *Globe*'s first great cause in the election campaign was the Redistribution Bill, one of the last bills passed before the session ended, during what the *Globe* thereafter referred to as "that last awful week". The Redistribution Bill was drawn up by a two-party committee (five Conservatives, three Liberals) and after nearly a year of work in committee had changed some riding boundaries with the net effect of adding four new seats in Toronto and four in Northern Ontario, raising the House from 98 seats to 106.

A front-page *Globe* cartoon showed Premier Whitney unveiling a large portrait of a sneaky-looking man with a scroll under his arm bearing the title "Gerrymander". The headline said: "Premier Whitney unveiling the portrait of his ideal". The cutline underneath read: "Gladstone, Disraeli, Washington, Lincoln and the rest—they're simply not in it for real statesmanship with Elbridge Gerry." The term gerrymander had been a dirty word in politics for nearly a century. It came from a combination of the words Gerry and salamander. As governor of Massachusetts in 1812, Elbridge Gerry had redrawn electoral boundaries arbitrarily to give his party an unfair advantage over his opposition. The Ontario redistribution, said the newest Liberal leader, Alexander G. MacKay, was "a straight gerrymander . . . fall-fair faking and a pea-under-the-shell racket".

He said equalization of population had been the avowed purpose of the new bill, but "only where political advantage was to be gained had the cry of equalization been raised for the obvious purpose of gerrymander." Whitney had used a slogan in speeches, claiming that he was "Honest enough to be bold, and bold enough to be honest". MacKay repeated this sarcastically as he zeroed in on one seat, Peel, where he said a couple of Tory communities had been taken off an adjoining constituency and added to Peel to make it possible to beat the sitting Liberal, John Smith, "and make it a safe Tory seat." (Cheers from the Conservative benches.) In its report, the *Globe* paraphrased the Whitney slogan as: "He has shown himself to be bold enough to be dishonest, and dishonest enough to be bold."

The *Globe*'s enthusiasm for A. G. MacKay was natural enough, considering one thundering election editorial that began: "The supreme necessity is a Liberal legislature."

But it could not have been easy, nevertheless, for the *Globe* to write that "Mr. MacKay has made a splendid record in public life."

This Owen Sound bachelor lawyer had taken over the Liberal leadership in September 1907. Ross, the loser in 1905, had gone to the Senate after bowing out in favour of the Hon. G. P. Graham. Graham subsequently was invited to join Sir Wilfrid Laurier's Dominion cabinet in the major portfolio of Railways and Canals (railroad-building was the major spending activity of the time). MacKay, leading a coterie of 27 Liberals against Whitney's 70 Conservatives, had an odd political background. In the general election of 1902 he won Grey North, but the election was declared void because of questionable election practices. He won again in a re-run in 1903, but again it was protested, and a seven-day trial led to so many subsequent adjournments that the matter was never resolved. With an election imminent, Premier Ross appointed him Commissioner of Crown Lands on November 22, 1904, just in time to adjudicate a thorny argument that was to reverberate through Ontario politics for years (including the 1908 election).

The dispute, as mentioned in Chapter Two, was over mining claims near Cobalt. The disputants on one hand were a millionaire contractor, Michael J. O'Brien of Renfrew, and his partner, a lawyer named James Brock O'Brian of Toronto. On the other were arrayed Noah and Henry Timmins, Duncan and John McMartin, and David Dunlap, Cochrane's brother-in-law. MacKay had heard the arguments and on December 20, 1904, in the midst of an election campaign, ruled in favour of the big Liberal M. J. O'Brien. (The O'Brien mine, within a few years, was returning a net profit in the millions.)

However, then came the 1905 election and the Ross government's defeat. In the early weeks of the Whitney administration the O'Brien-O'Brian title had been confirmed. But the Timminses, the McMartins, and Dunlap did not give up. They continued to seek evidence to back up their claim to the rich mine, and Dunlap moved to have the cabinet—which by now included his brother-in-law, Frank Cochrane—set aside the original award. Late in 1906 the matter was settled again (except for purposes of political platforms). At that time one wild but widely believed rumour about Cochrane's new mining tax was that it would not be on net profit but would be 20 per cent of the value of ore at the pithead. The *Globe* reported that in light of this rumour, and to clear away the legal tangle now surrounding the mine (by then valued at $10,000,000) O'Brien was offered a deal by the government. The government would stop its investigation and give him clear title to the mine, if he would agree to pay 25 per cent of the value of ore at the pithead, annually. O'Brien accepted.

What wasn't known generally at the time was that the Timmins-McMartin-Dunlap group later received a small sweetener. The cabinet had decided that the losers deserved something, too. After all, they had assembled much of the information on which the government had based its inquiry, leading to such a rich settlement. So the cabinet awarded the group, of which Cochrane's in-law, Dunlap, was the leader, $130,000 for its pains.

The *Globe* made much of this in its election campaign, calling it "The Brother-in-law Grant", and using it constantly to assail Cochrane. Then, on May 2, another anti-Cochrane issue turned up fortuitously in a *Globe* scoop from a Liberal nominations meeting in North Bay, headlined: "A Dismissed Registrar is Hunting Minister of Mines".

On accepting the Liberal nomination in Nipissing, John Loughrin told a hair-raising tale of a deal that had preceded the Liberal decision not to oppose Cochrane in East Nipissing in 1905. This was after Lamarche resigned, when the Liberal decision not to field a candidate gave Cochrane his seat by acclamation.

Backed by another Liberal lawyer, A. G. McGaughey of North Bay, Loughrin said that in 1905 he had been registrar and magistrate in Nipissing, but was willing and even eager to run against Cochrane. He had won the seat once before, and had been beaten narrowly (63 votes) by Lamarche—a result largely due, he said, to Lamarche's appeal to French-Canadian voters. But, stated McGaughey and Loughrin at the 1908 nominations meeting, back there in 1905 when Loughrin had been all ready to oppose Cochrane, Cochrane himself had handed McGaughey a letter promising that if Loughrin did not run, he would be allowed to keep his job as registrar (which, as part of the political spoils system of the time, normally might be turned over to a good Conservative as a result of the Whitney victory). So, said Loughrin, he did not contest the seat. But he had been fired anyway and his job given to Lamarche.

He produced another bombshell, largely reported in the *Globe,* when he stated

You will be surprised, perhaps, when I tell you that I was offered $8,000 in J. R. Booth's office in Ottawa, at the time Whitney called Cochrane to the Cabinet, if I would not oppose Cochrane's election in East Nipissing. I refused the bribe but [later] consented to keep out of the way if my position as registrar was not interfered with.

Cochrane's reaction was to write the following reply and send it by messenger to the *Globe*:

I enclose you a statement which I ask you to insert in your paper of Monday next, and in as prominent a place as your report in today's paper of the North Bay meeting.

Yours,
F. Cochrane.

The statement read:

The statements made by Lawyer McGaughey and John Loughrin in reference to me as published in the Globe of to-day are made out of whole cloth and with no shadow of foundation.

Unless the statements are retracted the parties who made them will be afforded an opportunity of being heard in the Courts.

The *Star* picked up the story later in the day. Loughrin, said the *Star*, refused to say who in Booth's office (Booth was a rich timber magnate) had offered him the $8,000 bribe. The *Star* also reported that Loughrin had something to say about the fact that Cochrane this time was not contesting the Nipissing seat. "Cochrane was afraid to face me in this constituency, but picked out the soft mark of Sudbury, where he will probably get a surprise." Both McGaughey and Loughrin said that the 1905 letter from Cochrane promising to see that Loughrin kept his job would be produced at the proper time.

Cochrane's denial to the *Toronto News* expanded on what he had told the *Globe*: The allegations were absolutely false,

he said, ". . . and as to the statement credited to Mr. Mc-
Gaughey that they had a letter from me that Mr. Loughrin
would not be dismissed in event of my election by acclamation,
and that the letter would be produced, I say that no such letter
was ever written by me and consequently cannot be produced.
Any letter of that kind alleged to be written by me is a
forgery."

About ten days later, with the *Globe* and other Liberal
papers making hay against Cochrane with this, and the
Brother-in-law Grant, and the Cobalt Lake lawsuit, Mc-
Gaughey turned up in Toronto and called upon local newspapers. He had with him the letter. It was not addressed
to him or to any Liberal, as he had been quoted earlier, but
to J. M. McNamara, president of the Conservative Association
at North Bay, and read:

> Dear Mr. McNamara:
> You ask what is the policy of the present Government
> with regard to the civil service and office holders
> appointed by the old Government.
> As to the offices that fall in from year to year, our
> political friends will naturally be preferred for the new
> appointments.
> Certain other offices, such as license inspectors, have
> been deliberately changed because we were convinced
> that this work should be done by officers in sympathy
> with the policy of the Government.
> As to sheriffs, registrars, crown attorneys, police
> magistrates and officers in like important positions, the
> Government would not dismiss without cause, and by
> this is meant opportunity for a hearing will be given
> to the person affected.
> Yours very truly,
> (Signed) F. Cochrane.

The *News* (certainly more of a Conservative organ by now,
and a few weeks earlier rumoured to have been bought by
Cochrane and E. B. Osler—a rumour that Cochrane denied)
quickly noted five words in the last paragraph—"would not

dismiss without cause"—and discovered that Loughrin had been dismissed following an investigation by the mining commissioner for the area, when he admitted having taken part in political campaigns. This was scarcely a secret, as he had been a defeated candidate (by Lamarche). No one at that time seemed to remember that the matter had been reported in just those terms (but in a milder way) in 1905.

The *Globe* headlined its new story on the matter: "A Chance for an Interpreter—Why Did Hon. F. Cochrane write this letter? McGaughey has nothing to withdraw".

The *Globe* printed the text of the Cochrane letter given above. One matter of obvious import was that Cochrane's letter was general, was addressed to the local Conservative president, and made no specific promises about Loughrin. McGaughey explained these matters for the *Globe* in this statement:

> The circumstances under which his letter was written are as follows: Chas. Lamarche was elected representative from East Nipissing by a majority of sixty-three in the general election of 1905. He later resigned to make way for F. Cochrane and this opened up the constituency. Mr. Lamarche had obtained his election on strong political argument that the French-Canadians should have a representative in Parliament. Many of his supporters were greatly incensed at his making way for Mr. Cochrane, and the Liberal Association called a convention to place a candidate in the field. Mr. Cochrane had been defeated a short time before [actually, three years before] in West Nipissing and was just recovering from a very serious accident.
>
> He came to North Bay the morning of the convention and interviewed the President of the Liberal Association. Mr. Loughrin had already represented the constituency in several Parliaments, and he is a very popular man, and he was ready unless assured of his position to resign and contest the constituency. Mr. Cochrane was informed of this. He was coming into a constituency where Mr. Loughrin had at one time carried by 790 of a majority, and where the Conservative candidate

had been elected in a three-cornered fight by a small majority of 63. He had an interview with Mr. A. H. Young, President of the Liberal Association, to whom was given the letter, a copy of which is enclosed.

The letter was purposely addressed to the President of the Conservative Association, but was written, I am informed, in North Bay and delivered to the President of the Liberal Association to be read at the convention.

On the reading of this letter before the convention it was stated that Mr. Cochrane did not wish to have it appear that he was making personal arrangements, so far as Mr. Loughrin was concerned; that what Mr. Loughrin had done up to that time would be cleared off the slate, and that so long as Mr. Loughrin remained in his office and attended to his duties he would be permitted to retain his position. On this statement, and on the strength of the letter, Mr. Cochrane secured his election by acclamation, and a short time later Mr. Loughrin was dismissed.

The *Star,* although supporting the Liberals, covered the McGaughey visit with what appears to have been a lively scepticism on certain points.

"And the letter you have talked about?"

"That was addressed to the president of the Conservative Association."

"The Conservative Association?"

"Yes, that was the way it was done but it was handed to the President of the Liberal Association. He read it at our convention. It was not intended to be made public, and it would not have been had Mr. Cochrane kept faith and not dismissed Loughrin."

"Did it covenant that no officials were to be dismissed if Mr. Cochrane were not opposed?"

"No, it merely said that no officials were to be dismissed."

"Then the understanding as to opposition being withdrawn was . . . ?"

"It was verbal."

"There was such an understanding?"

"There was."

"But it was not put to the letter?"
"No."
Mr. McGaughey says that he wants Mr. Cochrane to withdraw his denial. As to the contests in Northern Ontario, he declares that there are good prospects for electing Liberals in both Nipissing and Temiskaming.

The *Mail and Empire* (Conservative) merely printed the text of the Cochrane letter and rumbled that the letter in itself was "sufficient answer to the assertions of John Loughrin . . . for it is general in its character." It also recalled that when Mr. Loughrin had been a member of the legislature he had supported resolutions "which specifically asserted that partisan conduct at elections was sufficient grounds for the removal of an official from his post."

Especially, of course, if his party lost.

Meanwhile, the election campaign hummed along. On April 29 Whitney finally had made the date known: June 8. It would be the first Monday election in Ontario history. It turned out that one reason for the delay in making the decision (at least, this was the formal reason) had been to allow Frank Cochrane to tour the North and ascertain whether voters lists were ready in the new or altered constituencies. Obviously Cochrane did more throughout April than check voters lists. He was in the North from the middle of April on. In Haileybury, the *Haileyburian* carried an editorial saying that Temiskaming would be proud to have Frank Cochrane as its candidate—and that he should be returned by acclamation. A few days later he was nominated for Nipissing, but he turned the nomination down (clearing the way for Harry Morel, a Mattawa merchant—and also making it possible later for John Loughrin to state that Cochrane was ducking an encounter with him). When it became plain that Cochrane was going to run in the new riding of Sudbury, the conclusion in one weekly, *The Speaker*, was that it was fitting, for Sudbury was his old home town.

Cochrane seemed to leave a trail of confident Tories behind

him as he travelled through the North. Bob Shillington, a former noted Ottawa athlete, who was a mine owner and broker, was nominated for Temiskaming, and Cochrane spoke ("in a manner terse and convincing", reported the *Haileyburian*) for him at meetings in Cobalt and Haileybury. He hammered away a day or two later in Latchford, near Sudbury. While speaking and checking party organizations along the way, he was aware of a steady diet of anti-Cochrane and anti-Mining Act material from his old adversary at the *Sudbury Journal*, including a note that he had been wise not to contest Temiskaming, "as the Liberals have brought out a winning candidate in the person of Mr. A. A. McKelvie of New Liskeard."

Meanwhile, from Toronto a *Globe* dispatch reached the North and was reprinted in many papers, with either approval or disapproval, to the effect that Cochrane had declined the Temiskaming nomination because "it was hardly possible that he could have been returned for that electoral district, and by a great many Conservatives his defeat at Sudbury is also expected."

Commented the *Sudbury Mining News*: "No doubt it will be interesting for the people of Sudbury to learn that Mr. Cochrane's defeat is looked for, more particularly as at present there is no opponent in sight."

Back in Toronto, however, the *World*'s correspondent had called Cochrane's tour of the North a great success: "Looks Like Solid North" was the headline.

Cochrane returned to Toronto and reported to Whitney that the North was as ready as it would ever be. Whitney then set the election date. Cochrane returned to Sudbury for, at long last, a talk with his own local organization. The *Mining News* reported that he gave an account of his recent travels, "although somewhat hoarse". No wonder.

Still, he went on to Sault Ste. Marie to speak on behalf of William Hearst, the friend who later would succeed him as mines minister, and ultimately would become premier. Then

to Toronto, reading the *Globe* on the way to the effect that
"The Whitney government are already judged and doomed",
and that "Liberals all over the province are aroused to a pitch
of enthusiasm which augurs well . . ."

That was the day the Loughrin-McGaughey story broke. A
few days later Cochrane was on the platform behind Whitney
when the Conservatives opened their campaign in Hamilton—
the campaign that many of them had already been fighting for
nearly a year. Whitney set a tone immediately that seemed
designed to infuriate the *Globe*. Everything the *Globe* had
been complaining about, Whitney brought up cheerfully with
a remark that was to become a trademark throughout the
campaign: "I'm not here to defend that, I'm here to boast
about it."

The *Globe* hammered away both editorially and in its news
columns, castigating the Conservatives for "an incurable extravagance of language", repeating rumours of "a corrupt
campaign fund" based partly on kickbacks on grants made to
the Canadian Northern, bringing up the Brother-in-law Grant
time and time again, and blasting the Conservatives for an
election pamphlet on mining practices under the Ross government and calling it slander. On May 14, Cochrane finally got
back to Sudbury and accepted the unopposed nomination
there. He promptly loped off again to cover the North once
more and on May 16, on the letterhead of his hardware store
(F. Cochrane Importer and Dealer in Hardware, Lumber and
Mining Supplies a Specialty), he wrote to Whitney:

> I am glad to inform you that on going over the
> ground everything looks remarkably well. They [the
> Liberals] are making great efforts some places but have
> a hard time to create much enthusiasm.
> I am leaving tomorrow, Sunday, night for South
> Renfrew, and I intend to be on Monday in Eganville
> and Arnprior on Tuesday and later in Nipissing, for
> Morel. I intend leaving for the West after that, and
> expect to reach Port Arthur and Fort William on Satur-
> day and Monday . . . [He then raised some specific
> Lakehead issues and continued,] If I could state when I

arrive at Port Arthur, that those questions had been submitted, I feel that we might get things running the right way there.

Whitney replied at length, giving Cochrane the information (all on relatively local concerns) that he desired and adding, "You do not speak as if you intended coming here before you go to Port Arthur. I cannot say that it is necessary [but] if you can manage it we would be glad to see you." Cochrane, however, had his schedule and it was all in the North, with results that he seemed to smell already.

In the south, the *Globe* began on May 18 a series of what the editor called "political sermonettes" by Liberal Leader MacKay. There were eighteen publishing days left before the election, and he had that front-page space every day. Far from being abashed, the *Globe* hailed this technique of turning itself into a political handbill as being "never before seen in Britain or America".

But the long road of 1908's campaign was almost over. The *Sudbury Journal* called it political bribery when Cochrane went around the country promising that Hearst soon would join him in the cabinet. Sir Wilfrid Laurier unwittingly scuppered a tiny anti-Conservative issue by stating in the House of Commons question period that he had never heard of a Northern Ontario secession movement. "It is news to me," he said. The *World* and the *Globe* engaged in tedious arguments about the O'Brien mine dispute, explaining it to each other patiently in diametrically opposed terms. Cochrane in Sudbury had to wait for applause to subside every time he stood up and tried to speak. The *Christian Guardian* asked in a headline: "Is There No Better Way?" and said that in the election, misrepresentation and unfairness on both sides had overstepped the bounds of decency. The Hon. H. S. Blake wrote a 3,000-word eulogy of the Whitney government which the *World* published, although who could struggle through it would be difficult to guess. The *Sudbury Journal* said Cochrane supporters had been talking about a big majority, then a small majority, and now would be happy to get any majority.

The *Toronto Telegram* suddenly turned on Cochrane, called him a reactionary, and said that praise for him was written on "dusty and fly-specked tissue paper flowers of rhetoric" by those "ludicrous . . . Sifton-worshippers" at the *Toronto News*.

But then finally June 8 came, and with it the *Globe*'s last big salvo—a special story from Hamilton, front page, with huge headlines, trumpeting: "Ballots for Sale!"

The story said:

> This is a story of tampering with the ballot box which proves that the proud boast of Whitney re clean ballots, pure elections, was written in water . . .

It was a nice summer day, all over Ontario. Election workers struck a lively pace, trying to get voters to the polls before the 5 p.m. closing. In Sudbury that night the results came in to Lennon's Hall, Conservative headquarters, by a special wire from the returning officer. The crowd was big and good-natured, and a local group called Marsicano's Orchestra played during the intervals between poll reports.

Cochrane was on the platform scanning each report as it came in—not only from local polls, but from across the province. The *Mining News* reported

> . . . his face wore a continual smile, which occasionally broke into a joyous laugh accompanied by a shout when another gain was announced.

In the end, his majority in Sudbury was a comfortable 30 per cent over Liberal C. V. Price. When his election was assured and he walked out of the hall, reported the *Mining News*, ". . . he was captured, placed in a carriage, and drawn around town by a host of admirers."

But that wasn't all. When Ontario woke up the next morning, it was to news of the biggest electoral landslide in the province's history. The Conservatives had 87 seats, up 17. Every seat in Cochrane's North had gone Conservative. The Liberals had 18 seats, down 9.

The *Globe*'s story began: "Napoleon spent several years of his life explaining Waterloo."

CHAPTER SEVEN

One of the basic tenets of politics—or perhaps of life itself—
is that spectacular success instantly breeds requests to do it
again, bigger and better. Which is how it happened that four
months after Cochrane had delivered the solid North to the
Whitney victory, as well as helping in other parts of the
province, he was near the climax of yet another election. The
rink at Sudbury on a Friday night early in October was
tumultuous with all the hullabaloo of zero-hour politics. Frank
Cochrane had stood up and was looking out over a crowd of
more than 1200. Behind him on the platform was Robert
Borden, having his second try at beating Sir Wilfrid Laurier
at the polls. For five weeks, Borden had been working his way
across the Maritimes and through Quebec in a campaign
charging scandal and corruption against the Liberals. When
he reached Ontario at Pembroke on September 21, he shook
hands with Frank Cochrane, renewing an acquaintanceship
that had started in the 1904 federal campaign. But now he
knew more about Cochrane, and the two men had hit it off
well immediately. They thought alike. Borden's first exposure
to the House of Commons in 1896 had led him to write that
he was disappointed, because "methods were unbusinesslike

and waste of time enormous." Cochrane's businesslike, no-nonsense approach to politics was close to his own. Besides that, there was the record: no man ever had the hold on Northern Ontario that Cochrane had developed. In the twenty days after that September 21 election rally in Pembroke, Borden spoke at thirty-seven Ontario meetings—and in almost all, Cochrane was with him. The one in Sudbury was near the peak of Borden's Ontario campaign. Flags and bunting on the platform floated above the major political figures there to speak. Laurier's campaign slogan was, "Let Laurier finish his work." On one side of this Tory meeting a streamer proclaimed: "Laurier, Sifton [a controversial Laurier minister] and McCool [the local Liberal member] will finish their work on October 26." On the other side another streamer carried the contrapuntal message: "Borden, Gordon and Smyth will commence their work on October 27."

George Gordon was the Conservative candidate for Nipissing. W. R. Smyth was moving from the Ontario legislature to try federally in East Algoma.

The rink hummed with noise, a local orchestra alternating with a local military bugle band. A particularly large number of women were in the crowd. The bands had fallen silent when Cochrane rose, and when the applause for him ended he went through a few preliminaries and then Borden spoke for an hour and a half.

The opinion that the ruling federal Liberals were very much on the defensive in that campaign seems unanimous. In Borden's memoirs he remarks that "From 1904 to 1908 the Government had made an unfortunate and indeed evil record; extravagance and corruption had run riot in some of the departments. Public opinion had been profoundly disturbed . . ." Sir Wilfrid seemed to acknowledge something of the sort in a letter he wrote to Governor General Lord Grey a few days before the election. He thought the Liberals would win, "but I am not altogether pleased. I do not think there was sufficient justification for the nasty fight that has been put up by the opposition, but it has brought to light some things which are not pleasant and which must be gone into with a severe hand when the issue is settled."

In other elections Laurier always had some grand national scheme to use as a platform; in this one he had none, except a plea that he be allowed to finish his work. But this too had been turned against him in streamers such as the ones Cochrane had mounted over the platform in the Sudbury rink, by adding the election date to the Liberal slogan. And on the day before the Sudbury meeting a savage cartoon by N. McConnell was published in the *Toronto News*. The cartoon showed Laurier, his coat off and his sleeves rolled up, working over a scrubbing board in a laundry tub, with a pail labelled Soft Soap at his side. He was washing dirty linens labelled "Timber deals", "Marine and Fisheries scandals", "Western land deals", and other short phrases describing contentious matters of the time. Behind him in a doorway stood a man representing Canada, who was saying, "I think it would be cheaper to get a new housekeeper and new linen, than to let Laurier take another five years to clean up."

Not all the dirty linens were in Laurier's tub however. Cochrane was under fire for his campaigning methods. A. E. Dyment, the Liberal incumbent in Algoma East, acknowledged in a letter to Laurier that his Conservative opponent, W. R. Smyth, "will poll hundreds of votes more than anyone else they could have brought out . . ." Cochrane had persuaded Smyth to run and apparently didn't leave it at that. When Smyth beat Dyment, Dyment wrote to Laurier giving this reason for defeat:

> Cochrane, the Minister of Lands and Mines, was de-
> termined to defeat me by fair means or foul, and he
> simply held a gun at the head of every man, Lumberman,
> Hotel Keeper and Fisherman, who has any business what-
> ever with the Ontario Government. When a big Lum-
> bering Concern was found to be working for me, he
> would go personally to the Owner or Manager and tell

him, [without] making any bones about it, that he would throw his limits open for settlement, if he did not support my opponent. Hotel keepers were afraid to be seen speaking to me, and the Orange Lodges met about a week before Election Day and finished the trick.

Similar sentiments were expressed by James Conmee, the Liberal who had been beaten by J. B. Klock (with Cochrane's help) in 1896. Conmee was running in Thunder Bay–Rainy River and on October 23 he fired off a telegraphed critique of Cochrane's campaigning methods, addressing it to the Lieutenant-Governor, J. M. Gibson, at his home in Hamilton:

Mr. Cochrane, minister of lands and mines for Ontario, is intimidating a large number of voters both in the districts of Thunder Bay and Rainy River. The Mill owners, contractors and others who are entitled to permits for the cutting of timber are threatened with refusal of their permits in some cases, in other cases they are threatened with cancellation of permits unless they support the conservative candidate. Similar intimidation is being practiced with the knowledge of said minister by certain homestead inspectors who are coercing the settlers with cancellation of their homestead. In other cases where title of the lands had been previously refused they are now promised that title will issue to them if they support the conservative candidate. The said minister has himself been a party to this. The woodsmen should, in this northern section, have their permits for season renewed or granted respectively in September, but the permits are being suspended over their heads to intimidate them. None have yet been issued to these whom it is intended to intimidate in this way. Cochrane has himself written a letter forbidding certain steamship owners to operate their vessels on Nipigon lake. This is an act not only of intimidation but of usurpation of authority, as the provincial Government cannot prevent navigation on such waters. It is also stated that a large number of provincial constables have been appointed and that they are being used for the purpose of unduly intimidating voters by threats and otherwise. This corrupt and tyrannical action with respect to timber licenses is causing much loss. It has kept men out of employment and is causing depression and injuring the laboring classes, the lumbermen and the merchants. I appeal to you to put a stop to this conduct on the part of your minister.

James Conmee.

On October 24, Whitney told Gibson he had brought the matter to Cochrane's notice by telegram.

Voting day was October 26. Conmee won. His charges might have helped. Four days later Whitney told the Lieutenant-Governor that Cochrane "denies positively all the Conmee allegations" except the one about his forbidding certain steamship owners to operate their vessels on Nipigon Lake. Cochrane, wrote Whitney, had this right under the Forest Reserves Act, 61 Victoria, Chapter 10, and "In pursuance of this, written notice was sent by Mr. Cochrane to a steamboat owner or operator who was violating the law. With regard to the general statements, if the Minister has been in any sense guilty, he can be held accountable in the Courts."

Conmee didn't follow up his charges but had something in at least one area: special constables working around the polls. A quiet inquiry two months later resulted in Hearst's reporting to Whitney that two special constables, Phil Coyne and Charles Taylor, had combined their police duties with acting as scrutineers for W. R. Smyth in Algoma East.

With Ontario Conservatives apparently on the rise (buoyed by Whitney's June win) the federal election seemed to be touch and go. Later Laurier and Borden apparently agreed on one matter that might have done much to maintain Laurier's strength on polling day. Without it, Borden thought, Laurier wouldn't have had a working majority. Laurier noted the incident, disapproved of it, but failed to stop it. The incident was simply this: Some Ontario Conservatives who were members of the Orange Order and, Borden wrote, "whose zeal outran their discretion", printed a pamphlet exhorting Protestants to vote against Laurier because he was Catholic and French.

Joseph Schull noted in his biography of Laurier: "Sharp-eyed Liberal organizers seized on the material joyfully and [distributed] it through Quebec as the opinion of Robert Borden." Wrote Borden in his memoirs: "It did not have my sanction and I should have unhesitatingly forbidden its preparation and publication had I known of it. . . ." The first he knew of it was hearing a Liberal speaker denounce its publication. But by then the campaign was in its last days. Borden was in Halifax, and had no way of dealing with the anti-Borden wave that was sweeping Quebec and French-speaking regions of Ontario in the wake of the fake pamphlet. He was told later that "at many polling booths, Catholic priests, who had hitherto supported the Conservative party, stationed themselves with this pamphlet and besought members of their flock to cast their vote against a party that had resorted to such unworthy appeal."

When the votes were counted, Conservatives had increased their number of seats from 73 to 85, three of the gains being in Cochrane's North. The Liberals dropped from 139 to 133. The Liberal majority was reduced to 45 (there were three independents) over all and to a meagre 4 outside of Quebec. Laurier's share of the national popular vote was only 24,117 more than Borden's. But the Liberals stayed in power. So Cochrane's first major excursion into the national political realm had resulted in gaining three northern seats from the Liberals—Algoma East (W. R. Smyth), Nipissing (George Gordon), and Parry Sound (James Arthur), while holding Algoma West and failing to topple the Liberals only in Thunder Bay–Rainy River.

The results were bad enough that less than three weeks later Laurier decided privately to resign. He wrote his resignation and made an appointment to see Lord Grey to present it. But in the next couple of hours he was talked out of it. The man he wanted to succeed him, William S. Fielding, pointed out strongly that Laurier, not the party, had won the election; that Quebec had put them back into power because of

Laurier alone; and that he, Fielding, could not hope to hold Quebec. In short, Laurier's going would be a disaster to the party. Laurier tore up the resignation, cancelled his appointment with Lord Grey, and went back to his normal road—a road that now was leading, he knew, to another showdown with Borden, although Laurier hoped that political circumstances would be such that another leader would have taken his place safely at the head of the Liberals before then.

Because of the federal campaign, Cochrane hadn't had much time to savour the June victory in Ontario. Now he did. To the rest of the country it had been Whitney's triumph, but to the North it had been, as the *Sudbury Mining News* headlined its election report, "Mr. Cochrane's Victory". And in the *North Bay Tribune* the headline on the day after the election had been "Cock O' The North". Cochrane, with an hour between trains on his route to Toronto, had been met at the North Bay station by what the *Tribune* called an "en masse" welcome. A torchlight procession headed by a band wound through town looking for a place to stop. "No hall in town was large enough," reported the *Tribune*. So Cochrane had appeared on the first-floor balcony of the Queen's Hotel to speak to the dense crowd packed on the street below.

When he reached Toronto, too, the reporters were waiting. It was recalled that in a Toronto speech during the Ontario campaign, Whitney asked the city for "a home guard". Toronto had replied by a clean sweep of eight Conservatives. The newspapers printed the official address read to Cochrane in North Bay the previous night, mentioning the Toronto "home guard" but adding: "A still larger home guard has been given you by your friends and admirers in Greater [Northern] Ontario." In an interview, Cochrane said the result of the provincial election was a response to the "petty and scandalous" campaign the Liberals had waged.

"I appreciate it very deeply as a judgment by men who know of the administration of the mining country, its freedom from pull and its aim to be strictly honest and straightforward."

He noted that every centre vitally interested in mining had given majorities to the provincial government, and that in Temiskaming, where he said the Liberal candidate, Alex McKelvie, "was a worthy and popular man", a majority was recorded against him. His kind words for McKelvie were fairly generous, considering that McKelvie had accused him of "vicious practices" during the campaign.

An oddity was that in the one seat lost under Cochrane's provincial jurisdiction, North Renfrew—the only seat in his group that was outside of the mining country—the beaten candidate was David A. Dunlap, his mining magnate brother-in-law.

With two strenuous election campaigns in the first ten months of 1908, Cochrane hadn't time for much else. While Laurier was agonizing over his desire to get out, and then slowly picking up the bait that the United States was offering in the way of reciprocal trade agreements (which were to be the major issue three years later), and while Borden was beating back, without much trouble, a challenge to his leadership that had developed from his defeat, Cochrane turned his back on the hustings for a while. His big corner office in Queen's Park once again saw him on a daily basis while he listened to deputations beginning to develop pressure for a road into the new silver fields at Gowganda. The cabinet, deciding upon a set of new townsites in the North, named one after him—Cochrane, on the National Transcontinental where the northbound Temiskaming and Northern Ontario Railway, the government road, would intersect it that fall. Late in November he travelled with the T. and N. O. commissioners and their chief engineer to the townsite for an auction of the first lots to be sold.

It was a sea of mud. This was cheerfully admitted by a *Toronto News* reporter who went in with 600 prospective buyers by special train to the auction. But in the next breath he wrote that Cochrane would have a better climate than Winnipeg (which isn't difficult), "and will resemble more

Paris or Berlin." Others apparently shared his warm impression
of the rolling country with its thick woods of white birch and
poplar surrounding a pretty lake that was situated in the
middle of the thousand-acre townsite. Five chartered banks
were among land purchasers, with the Imperial Bank paying
top price: $1,050 for a standard lot, 66 feet by 132 feet. In
all, 72 of the prospective buyers bought lots—many of them
buying more than one—in what the *Toronto News* called, with
more enthusiasm than accurate prophecy, "the coming metropolis of the North".

CHAPTER EIGHT

These men are not really criminals. They had simply
been caught. Possibly if some of us had been caught
and got our just deserts we might be in jail, too.
                Frank Cochrane,
                speaking in the Grand Opera House,
                New Liskeard, September 1910.

It is difficult to think of many major modern politicians who
would make the above general remark about seven hundred
convicts serving time for a variety of criminal offences, and
linking them, however tenuously, to politicians. (The applause
might be too obviously heartfelt.) But the Whitney government had established at Guelph a prison farm, the forerunner
of the present Guelph Reformatory. Most of the prisoners were
there for relatively minor offences. The North was badly in
need of roads, so the authorities simply selected two hundred
men to serve their time in the North, building roads. Some
settlers didn't like the policy. In New Liskeard and elsewhere
Cochrane was replying. He remarked that night in New
Liskeard that there had been a cry for increased jail accom-
modation in the North. Opening up a new territory, he said,
brought in an influx of young men. Young men away from

home were apt sometimes to be foolish. "Some of the young men along with me have been affected that way," he said, "and might have got into trouble if I hadn't been along to keep them in order." (Laughter.) But it was possible to employ prisoners for the benefit of the country only by unlocking them and letting them work. Then he let the iron show: "There has been criticism, but notwithstanding, the policy of the government will go on."

He pointed out at another meeting, in another town, another point in this system: that the prisoners, when they had finished their terms, were offered rail tickets back to their homes. But many chose to stay on as free men, at full salary, and go on building the roads alongside those who were still serving time.

Maybe his confidence in making a casual joke suggesting that he and some of his colleagues might have wound up in jail, too, if they'd been caught, is as good an example as any of his apparent sense of unassailability. It wasn't that the Opposition didn't sometimes try him out for size. The old Brother-in-law Grant still cropped up now and again in the legislature—but even here, Cochrane seemed scarcely disturbed. More often, his colleagues would become angry on his behalf and thump the desks and try the Speaker. One typical instance occurred on March 19, 1909, when the deputy leader of the Liberals, D. J. McDougal (East Ottawa), asked for an explanation of the so-called Brother-in-law Grant that had been such a thoroughly threshed-out issue in the previous election. Cochrane rose.

"The people settled that last June 8," he observed, causing Conservative members around and behind him to thump their desks with delight.

"Not at all," persisted Mr. McDougal. "The people did not understand. . . . One would think by reason of its peculiar character the Minister would want it cleared up."

Cochrane replied, "I am not accustomed to insinuations. State plainly what you mean."

"It is said that the Minister of Mines paid out this settlement money to a near relative of his," McDougal said.

"The provincial treasurer paid it out," Cochrane said.

McDougal retorted, with cynicism: "A magnificent specimen of clever repartee. Clever! Very clever!"

"Quite McDougalish, in fact," snapped Whitney, whose boiling point was never high. He characterized McDougal's question as "a puerile attempt to injure the Minister of Lands, to do which the member for Ottawa has not hesitated to wilfully misrepresent the facts."

McDougal angrily demanded that the premier withdraw that statement about misrepresentation.

Sir James did so, quite mildly for him. "I wish the honourable gentleman long life and happiness," he intoned. "But if he is ever placed in the situation of the Minister of Lands and Mines I trust he will be able, and as willing, to turn down a relative in the cause of the people of Ontario."

End of argument.

The style of the Whitney government through the entire period after its massive victory in 1908, especially in matters falling in Cochrane's bailiwick, was one of firmness and confidence. The Mining Act of 1906, with its revenue-producing adjunct in 1907 and subsequent housekeeping amendments, seemed to have been precisely what was needed to keep Ontario mining development moving along rapidly at the same time that the industry's value to the public purse increased every year. An indication of general acceptance by the industry was that by 1909 and 1910 petitions for changes in the Act had fallen off to a trickle. Mining growth was reflected in requests for more northern roads, and railroads. Here again Cochrane, who formulated cabinet policy on such matters, showed no inclination to respond unduly to pressure.

His recurring challenge was to pick a course between pleasing his northern constituents, and still not give away natural resources in wholesale lots. In March of 1909 a large delegation from Sudbury—most recent in a long stream of supplicants on this issue—saw Whitney and Cochrane to urge that the government help the Canadian Northern Railway extend its line from Sudbury to Port Arthur, with a branch to Gowganda. One member of the delegation was Charles Mc-Crea, a political protégé of Cochrane's (later to follow Hearst in Cochrane's original portfolio). A Port Arthur delegation was on hand too, urging its interests. Also, Sudbury delegates wanted $40,000 immediately for a wagon road to Gowganda, to start without delay.

The *Sudbury Journal* reported a few days later that the delegation "had not long to wait for an answer", but the *Journal* didn't like the answer at all:

> ... Before the session closed on Thursday the Premier announced the policy of the Government. No bonds will be guaranteed, or cash grant made, but a land grant of 4,000 acres of land per mile for the main line will be offered. This offer, however, has so many strings attached to it that it is doubtful if the promoters of the railway could raise one dollar from capitalists on the proposition. All pine and mineral of the grant remains the property of the Government and the land can only be sold at a price fixed by the Government, and at such a time as it insists that it shall be sold.
>
> The Premier admitted that the land was now valueless but he thought it a good plan to get the clay belt opened up and thus save the people having to spend $25,000,000 in building a road of their own.
>
> What the Government should have done was to guarantee the bonds of the Company, and keep the land, then when the clay belt was opened up and developed the country would reap the advantage.
>
> So far as can be seen the Government is making no effort to help the thousands of people who are now in the Gowganda country by making preparations to build either wagon roads or extending the T. & N. O. R'y. The supplies now going in are very little more than sufficient for those who are there. The present roads will be impassable in a few weeks [with the end of

winter] and it will be a case of starve or get out to a large number.

It looks as if the policy of the present Government is similar to that of the former—to get all that they can out of New Ontario and return as little as possible.

This decision on the Canadian Northern was challenged by Liberals in the legislature, using much the same derogatory terms as the *Journal*. But on the same day, March 31, the government announced a $50,000 appropriation for a wagon road to Gowganda. Did that mean, demanded Liberal Leader A. G. MacKay, no railroad? Cochrane replied that the government did not yet know whether Gowganda and nearby settlements that would be served by the road, including Smythe and Elk Lake City, would be permanent. Little was known about the country beyond surface conditions. Before committing the government to a costly railroad policy there, most careful attention would have to be given and abundant information obtained.

Within a few weeks, it became evident that even without a railroad, Gowganda was happy with the prospect of a road to replace the one then running through bush and over lake ice and usable only in winter. A sale of town lots was announced by Cochrane, and prices jumped high above those sold by auction only a month earlier, before the road was announced.

Cochrane spent a busy summer in 1909 without a vacation. Dr. Joseph O. Réaume, Minister of Public Works, was in poor health. Cochrane took over Public Works while Réaume sailed for Europe for three months to recuperate. In June Cochrane began arranging a tour of the North by special train, a repeat of a pet project he'd had in mind for some time—to take as many legislators as possible, with newspapermen and some guests, on a tour of what he always called Greater Ontario. Besides the fact that, as his secretary George Yates wrote in 1950, "he was ... never happier than when in the North country among the people and the life he knew and loved," his idea was that the more members knew about the North, the better treatment the legislature would give it. Also that summer he decided that the government should get out of the mining business. An experimental government-owned mine near Cobalt had been only a modest success. He announced its sale by tender, for cash and an ore royalty. This sold for $113,111, the highest bid received, and an equal amount was received for about 320 acres of mining property in the vicinity. At the same time he quickly made a decision of a type that would be impossible today. Fire had swept through 144 square miles of prime timber land in the Mississauga forest reserve. Burned timber is sometimes usable, but only if cut and milled immediately. Cochrane simply put it up for sale by tender. Imagine the uproar that would ensue today before any large provincial forest could be opened to timber operators, even for excellent cause and on a temporary basis. His reasoning was simple: insects quickly attack burned trees and finish the job of destruction. In a year the forest would be a total loss. Cochrane sold it, demanding that the timber be cut that year. The high bidder agreed to pay so much per thousand board feet cut, as well as an extra $2 a thousand as a government fee. In addition he was required to post a performance guarantee. A newspaperman who toured the North about that time pointed out at the conclusion of a long article in the *Toronto Star Weekly*: "You may travel pretty well over New Ontario and you will get a variety of opinions about the way that country is being administered. It is not all one grand sweet song of praise. . . . One thing they will tell you, though, and that is that Frank Cochrane is running things . . ."

That was the background on the night of Monday, September 6, when a train of five Pullmans, two diners, and two "special" cars (for "special" one might read "bar") eased out of Union Station in Toronto. This was the northbound Cochrane special, and, reported one of the half-dozen newspapermen along,

About 140 of the government's guests were on hand. It took them only a few minutes to get into their appointed places. In his home district the member of the legislature is a judicious mixture of wise dignity and geniality, but here the assumed wisdom was forgotten and the party might have been a Sunday School picnic so far as merriment was concerned. The Honourable Frank Cochrane roamed about with his hat a-tilt "joshing" his guests; the Honourable W. J. Hanna, who is a raconteur from Raconteursville, told stories to a large and hilarious audience. Col. Matheson unbent and "kidded" his friends [for hours, until] conversation flagged and snoring became fashionable. . . .

One may recapture approximately the feeling of this expedition only by imagining the Ontario of the time. Once the train chuffed northward out of what was called Old Ontario, the province was only a degree or two removed from wilderness. There were no clanging bells at highway crossings, because there were no highways in the sense that we know them today. There were few warm and welcome lights flickering in the countryside. A man running up the blind in his lower berth the next morning south of North Bay was looking at almost primeval bush, broken here and there by a collection of log shacks clustered around a railway water tower or a sawmill.

From several long accounts of this tour of September 1909, as well as others, Cochrane seemed to have three major purposes. Educating the legislators obviously was one; the region produced one-sixth of the province's annual income, and yet the small and scattered population felt alienated and ignored, and the secessionists always had fertile soil for their lively meetings, full of invective for the effete south. A second purpose was served by taking journalists and magazine writers along. They wrote long articles which in turn were picked up by other publications. Cochrane made sure that every settlement that had any agricultural activity at all trotted it out in the form of fall fairs for the visitors. Settlement was the big activity of the time, but plugging Northern Ontario as rich farmland wasn't easy, one problem being the railroads themselves, which ran land-settlement schemes on their huge land grants farther west, getting a profit, first by selling rail tickets, second by selling land, and third by establishing agricultural settlements that would support the railroad by freight shipments in and out. "The newspapers are all shouting of the West," Cochrane told an audience in the opera house at New Liskeard, "and yet the province of Ontario produces twice the farm wealth that is produced by the three new provinces of the West."

But the third purpose of such trips was also important. They were described as non-political, in that the town councils and boards of trade that arranged welcomes along the way were of both sides (there were only two sides then) of the political coin. But North Bay, Cobalt, Haileybury, Cochrane, Frederick House, Matheson, Englehart, New Liskeard, Latchford, Elk Lake, Montreal River, (wrote a correspondent on the 1909 trip)

> ... all these northern towns want something. It may be a concession that will disable the nearest rival town, it may be an expensive railroad spur, it may be better freight rates, it may be a change of government policy on timber or settlement, it may be a mining record office, or it may be nothing more than a few hundred feet of railway siding. But they all want something, so their honorables the Ministers of the Ontario government must walk softly in the North. ...

At each stop, while legislators and newsmen fanned off in several directions to inspect mines or timber work or farms, usually Cochrane and his secretary, George Yates, and another minister or two would hold court in the largest meeting-place in town so that citizens could trot out their requests and complaints, before the usual nighttime party or smoker. They were strenuous days and nights. As one journalist wrote,

> ... Haileybury was reached at seven o'clock and after

dinner the visitors were taken aboard steamers on Lake Temiscamingue and shown the town by night. It is an exceptionally pretty town, this Haileybury, and has a townsite immeasurably superior to that of Cobalt. Its natural beauties have made it the residential annex to the silver city, and street after street of fine houses are to be found here. Up in the north they call it Million-airetown because it houses so many of the men who have made their fortunes out of the mines.

Huge bonfires were lit along the waterfront of Hailey-bury and Port Cobalt and these along with the innumerable lanterns gave the town the appearance of a great city. Lord Charles Beresford [an English guest on the 1909 trip] was given an enthusiastic reception at the smoker that followed the lake trip and the committee on joyful noise provided a first-class program.

What with tramping around Cobalt and the festivities at Haileybury, they were weary legislators who crept into their berths that night, and sore of foot when on Wednesday morning at dawn the officials announced that there would be a short stay in Cochrane.

Some of the side trips were taken by canoe or boat. The few miles from Cochrane to Frederick House was done with the visitors standing wide-legged for balance on flatcars drawn by a slow-moving locomotive. The Englehart fall fair—the first ever and arranged especially for the occasion—covered only a one-acre lot,

> ... with various grains, fullheaded and of phenomenal height, displayed in racks in the open while the fat stock were tethered outside the fence. ... It was only a moment after arrival before Hon. Frank Cochrane was standing high on the top of a rail fence with a crowd gathered around him, haranguing the multitude in answer to its cheers.
>
> New Liskeard showed first grade hard wheat at its fall fair; 40 bushels to the acre we were told. And excellent vegetables were served to the legislative party for dinner as earnest of what the country can do under cultivation.

The party arrived at one town, Elk Lake, just after a visit

by liquor inspectors had clamped down on the local boot-
leggers, and hundreds of barrels were staved in and the

> ... beer added to the waters of the Montreal River,
> dismal testimony of the ruthlessness of the law.

But Elk Lake, which had grown in a year from four log
shacks to 2,000 men, and had to be reached by boat in summer
and by horse-drawn sleighs in winter, did produce another
memorable sight for the travellers:

> When the citizens entertained at a banquet that
> night, the approach to the big dining hall used by the
> miners was lighted by miners' candlesticks thrust into
> stumps making a lighted path to the door.

At a North Bay meeting on the final night the speeches lasted
so long before the entertainment began that the legislators had
to leave in the middle of the program. Reported the *Globe*:

> ... One more night in the train, a hilarious one for the
> juniors and a sleepy one for the older members, and
> the train pulled into Toronto. It was a history-making
> trip. Never before have members of the legislature
> had the opportunity of seeing the new North in shape
> for the settlers. It required a great deal of imagination
> a few months ago for them to realize the possibilities
> of the district, but with live towns springing up in
> every part and samples of agricultural wealth that
> promise in the end to be more valuable to Ontario than
> even the far-famed Cobalt, the representatives begin to
> realize the claims of Northern Ontario.

Obviously, Cochrane's decision to take along journalists had
made at least one *Globe* convert. One other correspondent,
D. Strachan, of a monthly publication called *The Presbyterian*,
was equally impressed—"except by the swearing I heard" and
by the sanitary conditions in Cobalt.

> ... They are simply infamous. The result is an epidemic
> of typhoid fever, simply because men will not be mindful
> of the ordinary laws of cleanliness. ... [However] I can't
> close these wayside impressions without a personal testi-
> mony to the man Ontario holds responsible for the

trusteeship of all that northern country, Hon. Frank Cochrane, Minister of Forests and Mines. To be the head of such a department is no sinecure. Even I was tempted to quietly hint to him, "I should like a few hundred miles of timber limits or a good paying mine for a small consideration, a very small one." But I didn't. I thought others might have hinted before me. I can conceive of many troubles he might have to contend with. But he impressed us all as a splendid man. Not a politician, but a man who knows the north, who loves the north, and believes in the north, and is working 24 hours a day that the untold treasures of the north may be preserved to the best interests of the people of Ontario. It is very delightful to mark everywhere the genuine respect of all classes for the man who is trying to administer their affairs that Ontario as a whole may be enriched.

Some tours were in the grand manner, especially the many in which he sought to interest British and American capital in helping to develop the North's vast hinterlands. But his favourite method of covering every corner of his bailiwick at least once a year seemed to be to take two or three ministers along, and move by private railroad car. If 1910 had been an election year, it would have been easy to impute short-term political motives. But in August and September that year Cochrane was seldom out of the North. He started with Agriculture Minister James S. Duff, Works Minister J. O. Réaume, and Provincial Secretary W. J. Hanna in Port Arthur with a midnight arrival on July 30. Their purpose was to survey ways to develop the North better and faster; and as their special car was dropped at Fort William, Rainy River, Nipigon, Fort Frances, it seems (from thousands of words of newspaper reports of the time) that every local problem known to man or beast was paraded before them. Cochrane's dry wit was beginning to be noticed. The *Toronto News* man, with him all the way (politically, by then, as well as physically), included this line in his Port Arthur dispatch:

. . . Mr. Cochrane said he was glad the meeting was

non-political because the members of the government
know no politics anyway except for a couple of months
every four years (applause) ...

And from Kenora, where the Board of Trade was asking
a ban on commercial fishing for fifty miles around, to restore
rod-and-line fishing for tourists:

> ... His breezy sincere way of meeting deputations and
> telling them plainly what he thinks of their requests
> has a rather refreshing air of novelty. There is nothing
> formal about these audiences, which proceed on the
> basis that every man is entitled to his opinion and the
> free expression thereof. Mr. Cochrane proceeds on the
> same theory himself and the man who "wants an answer,
> yes or no," usually gets it with promptness and dispatch.

One four-day period Cochrane and his party spent in the
Nipigon Forest Reserve. They travelled partly on a small
steamer provided by railway contractor and mine owner M. J.
O'Brien (a Liberal) through his brother on the spot, John
O'Brien, and partly by canoe with numerous chances to "test
the fishing qualities of the area" (as the *News* reporter deli-
cately put it).

> ... Mr. Cochrane was able to personally examine
> the timber adjacent to the lake and the river, to inspect
> the personnel of the fire-rangers, their quarters, and the
> manner in which the regulations of the Department are
> observed by tourists who make use of the various camp-
> sites.
>
> In this connection it may be mentioned that the
> Ministerial party met some American tourists making
> their way up the river. Shortly after landing for lunch
> at the campsite recently vacated by the Americans,
> a camp fire was found smouldering in plain view of one
> of the Department's printed notices to tourists to
> extinguish fires. The Minister sent the Chief Fire Ranger
> after the party with instructions to cancel forthwith the
> license of the chief guide, whose duty it was to see
> that the fire was extinguished before leaving, and to
> warn the others that a repetition of the offence would
> mean the cancellation of the licenses of the other guides

and the permits of the tourists as well, in which case a carefully planned fishing trip would come to a sudden termination.

In September he was back in the North again, with the fever epidemic still raging in Cobalt, once again touching all the bases in the mining and agricultural districts, inspecting, commenting, even kissing babies (the first child born in Cochrane was named for him). Each town's newspaper reported his visit at length, with full discussion of all the local issues. By the end of the month the job was finished for the moment: he had visited every major settlement and many minor ones in all Northern Ontario, and the only note of dissent was printed in the *Cobalt Nugget,* which had been fighting him steadily ever since its founding in 1908. The *Nugget* contended that secession

> will be the ultimate fate for New Ontario, and . . . the area will never get its just deserts until a new province has been created. The next dominion election in this section will undoubtedly be fought on this issue.

Having apparently brought a fair measure of peace to the mining industry, Cochrane set about making equally sweeping reforms in forest policy. Near the end of 1909, there was a furor in newspapers and public meetings over a plan to cut some timber in Rondeau Provincial Park near Chatham, and thus, some speakers charged, "lay waste to the only surviving vestige of big timber in Old Ontario". Kent County Council passed unanimously a resolution condemning this plan. Cochrane, in an interview with the *Globe*, replied in terms that were unusual at the time but are much more familiar in the 1970s in connection with other parks. What would happen at Rondeau was, in effect, a statement of a scientific forestry policy, he said,

> . . . carefully thought out after consultation with experts and practical foresters. It is designed solely to preserve in perpetuity the forest at its best.

> To my mind Rondeau Park is one of the finest pieces
> of natural forest in the province and our sole aim is
> to preserve and intensify its beauty and value. At present
> and for some time past its progress has been impeded by
> over-mature growth. In some cases the trees have died.
> Many have fallen, destroying others in their fall. Young
> growth has little opportunity for development. It is
> proposed to proceed wisely and carefully along the
> lines of approved forestry to perpetuate this beautiful
> natural forest. Nothing will be done to detract from
> its natural beauty. . . .

At the time, he was in the midst of drafting a new forestry
policy, with the principal groundwork being done by his
forestry deputy, Aubrey White. When announced in April it
was seen to follow closely the principles of his Mining Act.
More responsibility was demanded of timber operators. They
would be required to pay more royalties for the use of this
provincial resource. The government would take a much
stronger hand in seeing that rules were carried out.

The increased income to the province as a result of the new
policy was estimated at $300,000 annually, raising forest in-
come to about $1.5 million a year. All timber dues were
increased, ground rental was nearly doubled (still only to a
modest $5 a mile), and the timber operators would be required
to pay the total cost of fire-prevention work, including rangers'
salaries, with the government still the court of last resort in
supervision. Fire rangers in the past had been hired each year
as part of the patronage system. This would be ended, although
Cochrane said,

> . . . we will continue to require that their names shall
> be submitted here so that we may give them full
> instructions, and further, that we shall have the right
> to remove any man who neglects his duty and require
> the substitution of a new man in his place. We have also
> retained the right to require all licensees to put fire
> rangers on their limits. If they neglect to do so we are to
> have the power to put on the necessary rangers, and
> charge their wages and expenses against the operators,

withholding the license until these charges are paid. We also retain the right to appoint what are called supervising rangers, whose duty it is to see that the work is efficiently done. These will be placed in charge of certain districts, into which, for the convenience of supervising, the licensed territory will be divided. These supervisors will be furnished with lists of rangers appointed by each licensee and the limits they are on, and by visiting them frequently they will be able to see that the fire rangers are active in the performance of their duties.

One provision was that where timber limits had been leased years before, in perpetuity, the government claimed an interest in second-growth timber that might now be almost ready to cut.

Another innovation was a requirement that timber operators clean up after themselves. The debris normally left in the woods would no longer be tolerated, because the dry twigs and branches of discarded tree-tops made fires much more destructive. At the time, the *Montreal Witness* reported that Cochrane's insistence on having tree-tops cleaned up and burned safely in winter "will be watched with interest outside of Ontario, and if the results are satisfactory the methods will doubtless be imitated."

Toronto *Saturday Night* hailed the new policy.

> The Hon. Frank Cochrane is taking an attitude which entitles him to much credit among those who are making an attempt to introduce a policy of conservation of ... one of our greatest natural resources.

While Cochrane was travelling an estimated 6,000 miles in the North that year, covering every area including the new Porcupine Gold Camp (where he announced a 27-mile government-built railroad spur connecting to the T. and N. O.), a few descriptions reached print in newspapers and magazines of his methods of working.

> *Saturday Night*:
> It is easier to get in to see the Prime Minister than

to see the Minister of Forests, Lands and Mines. The crowds of lumbermen, mining sharks, and smooth party lawyers after concessions that troop down toward the corner room on the ground floor of the east wing are a sight to see. George Yates, the Minister's secretary, handles them all with a precision that only a newspaper training can give. He can pick out the good ones, and the shysters are pretty nearly always diplomatically steered out.

The Star Weekly:
Uncanny energy marks his work in the office. Before the merry morning charwoman has completed her task and long before the first clerk puts in an appearance, the Minister of Lands, Forests and Mines, comes striding in and settles down at his desk. The stenographer attached to his office and his secretary have given up the attempt to beat him down. As a matter of fact he does not want them to. He gets in some of his best work before the building wakes up and he is often in his office long after they have gone to sleep at night.

He is the hardest Minister in the building to get at. Not that he is any longer shy of the press, but there are usually half a dozen people waiting in his ante-room ahead of you, and he is quite capable of talking to any one of them for an hour if the subject interests him. His office is the place in which to look for types of the north, for the man with the shoe pack and corduroy is often there with a grievance or a suggestion, or a request. These recent changes in the timber dues have got him into hot water in some quarters, just as the raise in mining dues some time ago did. But his closest friends were hit over that and he didn't spare them, and they are none the less good friends because of it.

As a diplomatic statesman, Mr. Cochrane is a shining failure. There are two kinds of Minister; one of them tells you that your request is preposterous and that he won't ask the Government to waste its time over it, or else that it's all right and he'll do it. You know exactly where you are with that kind of a man, and you either want to smash the furniture or shake hands with him. The other kind promises serious consideration

and is so interested and sympathetic that you are confident he is going to help you. You smash the furniture
about six months later with this kind, when you find
that you haven't got even the consideration. Frank
Cochrane is an example of the former. He is about as
diplomatic as Sir James Whitney, and the latter knows
as much of diplomacy as a pile driver does about
beating eggs. The consequence is that the Minister of
Mines manages to get a lot of people in a blazing bad
temper at him every now and then. . . .

At the year's end, the *Toronto News* summed him up this
way:

Mr. Cochrane is never stampeded by the sensational
methods of individuals or organizations bent upon
getting the Government to assist them in accomplishing
their own ends. He has the strength quietly to study a
given situation, the ability to make up his own mind,
and the necessary weight within the Cabinet to get what
he wants done. He has shown much courage in dealing
with the lumber interests, and the possession of much
authority with his colleagues in getting his advanced
programme for the conservation of our forest wealth
well under way. Since he came into office the educational facilities of Northern Ontario have been greatly
increased. The extension of the Provincial Railway to
Porcupine camp is only one aspect of the forward policy
pursued in connection with the Government line. The
rich mineral discoveries of the Temiskaming country
have been so handled as to yield the treasury handsome
returns. One million dollars was secured for a single
lake-bed that under the previous government would
have fallen into some speculator's hands almost free of
charge. An increasing proportion of this revenue has
been returned to New Ontario in the shape of colonization roads, a greatly extended school system, and
adequate judicial machinery. The settler has been given
the mineral and timber on his land. The many water
powers not alienated by a former Administration will
remain under Provincial control as to the condition
of their use. Mr. Cochrane long since removed disputes

over mineral land titles from political control, and generally he has exhibited an unwearying and effective concern on behalf of his constituents, many of them sturdy pioneers whose energy has contributed much to the making of the north country.

CHAPTER NINE

If any lady who has married a political headlight wants
to know what kind of a man her husband is, we would
advise her to attend the meetings of the opposite party
to which he belongs. There she will learn that he drinks,
beats his wife, neglects his family, owes everybody and is
nothing but a whitewashed sepulchre, surging with
criminal desires, rejoicing in deeds of darkness committed
in the past.

Sudbury Journal, August 3, 1911.

At a conference of Conservatives held Saturday morning
in the Albany Club, Hon. Frank Cochrane announced
his acceptance of the permanent chairmanship of the
[party's] Dominion election committee for Ontario. His
name has been mentioned in this connection for some
time, and there is satisfaction in the Conservative camp
at his acceptance. He will be chief organizer in the
province for the coming federal elections.

Toronto World, August 7, 1911.

It is not known when Frank Cochrane and Sir Robert Borden
first met, but some signs point to the Ontario election of 1902.
Borden had been a political novice in Halifax when he first
was persuaded to run in the federal election of 1896. He was

elected, but the Conservatives under Sir Charles Tupper were beaten badly by Laurier. Borden tried to retire from public life in 1900 when another election was imminent, but Tupper in the meantime had decided that the quiet Halifax lawyer had a future in the party; he talked Borden into running again. Once again, on November 7, 1900, the Conservatives were beaten. Tupper was among the fallen but once again Borden won one of the two Halifax seats handily. When Sir Charles resigned as leader at the next party caucus in Ottawa on February 5, 1901, he proposed Borden's name.

This amazed Borden, he wrote later in his memoirs. He declined at first, but when the long caucus finally was adjourned until the following evening, Tupper went to work. Eventually Borden accepted but secretly specified that he would only serve one year. He was persuaded not to announce the temporary nature of his leadership because he was told it would tend to diminish his authority. This keeping secret the one-year provision turned out to be a sound idea; he was the Tory leader for nearly twenty years.

Soon after assuming the leadership he began to make forays into Ontario, speaking in Toronto, Lindsay, and other cities, often with James Pliny Whitney or other Ontario Conservatives on his platform. Cochrane already was a friend of Whitney and in 1902 attended some of these meetings with him, as Whitney's new hope for the North. Whitney lost that election narrowly, although with a small edge in the popular vote, but the relationship between him and Cochrane—and, more distantly, with Borden—continued in political activities until in 1904 Cochrane began to turn up regularly as a northern supporter on Borden's platforms. The smashing 1908 victory for the Ontario Conservatives brought the men much closer later that year when Borden was running his second losing federal campaign.

But by 1911, it was a new game entirely. Cochrane by then was the most influential Ontario Tory next to Whitney himself. As early as January 1906, Borden had begun a correspondence with Whitney stressing the importance of finding "a man of pretty big calibre" who could organize the province for both federal and provincial Tory campaigns. Cochrane, then a neophyte, was not mentioned. But on January 3, 1910, Whitney suggested Cochrane and Réaume to serve on Borden's Committee on Preliminary Arrangements for a Dominion convention of the party. Two days later he withdrew Cochrane's name, at Cochrane's request, but Borden demurred.

"So far as Cochrane is concerned," Borden wrote, "I think it especially important that he should represent the northern district as his work in that section was particularly active and effective during the last Federal campaign." Borden had Whitney and Cochrane to dinner in Ottawa a few days later, and on January 20 Borden and Cochrane both spoke at a dinner in Ottawa for delegates to the French Canadian Congress of Ontario. Borden to Whitney, January 21: "Mr. Cochrane had an excellent reception, and made a very tactful speech, which was received with great applause. He is evidently very well known to the delegates and has a strong hold upon them."

In the following year it became accepted that when the next federal campaign arrived, Cochrane would be detached from his Ontario ministerial duties for the more political role. Chairmanship of the Ontario section of the federal party meant that Cochrane sat in on party councils planning strategy for the whole nation. Taking on the double job of Ontario organizer made him the most important single backroom politician in the national party, because Ontario held the key to toppling Laurier.

There was nothing really very complicated about this feeling in 1911 that, given a campaign without unforeseen disasters, Laurier could be had. Ontario was the British-ties stronghold of Canada. And Laurier, who had specialized in winning elections on big nation-sweeping issues (except in 1908), this time picked one that backfired, although for a

time it seemed likely to sweep him into office with a b*
majority that ever.

The issue was reciprocity. In 1908 when William Taft
followed Theodore Roosevelt into the U.S. presidency, the
preceding sixteen years of the Republican policy of high
tariffs was wearing thin. Prices were high, and people felt
they could be lowered by allowing foreign goods in at lower
tariffs, or no tariffs at all. As this mood progressed in the
United States, and reciprocal deals were made with other
countries to facilitate imports to the United States as long as
the other countries would reciprocally lower tariffs on U.S.
goods coming in, Canada was a holdout—a prisoner, in a
sense, to a policy of giving Britain preferential trade treatment
almost across the board. But letters began to pass back and
forth between the two countries as the United States sought to
capture more Canadian trade with the offer of lowered tariffs
in return. Laurier's finance minister, William S. Fielding,
went to Washington and made a deal that really was the
tip of what was to come. The United States was threatening
a 25 per cent super-tariff against Canadian goods. But by
giving it preference on a group of minor trade items, Canada
persuaded the United States to stop waving its big stick.

In the next few months negotiators for both countries
worked at spreading this new accord. In December of 1910
and January of 1911 Fielding seldom occupied his seat in the
Commons; he was in Washington. What was shaping up,
wrote Joseph Schull in his biography on Laurier, "promised
free or almost free entry to the United States for Canadian
grain, meats, cattle, dairy products, lumber, pulpwood,
minerals, and fish. American duties would be lowered on a
sizeable list of Canadian manufactures, and little or nothing
was asked in the way of return. The tariffs protecting Canadian
industry were hardly to be touched. The imperial preference
was to remain and all the United States was to receive was a
general lowering of Canadian tariffs to the levels enjoyed
by other countries of the world. . . ."

When that was announced in the Commons on January 26, the first impact was crushing to Borden's Conservatives. He commented briefly that his party stood for reciprocity within the Empire, with no other trade alliances that would "prevent this greatest consideration" for the 300 million people under the British flag. But his members behind him were despondent. At caucus the following day one of his principal supporters, George Foster, said that when the proposals were presented "his heart had gone into his boots". Western members declared emphatically that they couldn't fight reciprocity and win an election. For years farmers had wanted this free trade north and south to supplant the long and expensive railroad haul east and west. One Western member even said he dared not vote against the government's reciprocity proposals when the vote came.

That was the time Laurier should have called an election. But then, wrote Borden later, a strange thing happened. Many of the Ontario members were in the habit of taking trains home on weekends. That weekend, they left despondently. The Toronto area members found the *Globe* hailing reciprocity as the greatest act of statesmanship since the invention of the gavel. Then they started talking to the people: the largely British-blooded ordinary citizens, who ran corner stores and were lawyers and drove streetcars and worked in the livery stables (Toronto still had a few, and smaller districts more). Cochrane was in the North that weekend, and the pulse that he knew so well up there concurred with the feeling in the south. He communicated this to George Gordon, the Nipissing M.P., and anyone else he could reach. The same process was going on all over the province, except in Ottawa, where the reciprocity euphoria still held sway.

It was a straight Britain-versus-the-Yanks feeling in Ontario. But it was intensified also by the same emotions that prompted Canadians, sixty years later, to form something called the Committee for an Independent Canada. Whatever happened, when the Ontario members returned to Ottawa at the first of the week, Borden wrote, "those who left Ottawa dejected and wavering came back confident and strong in their opposition to the government proposals." He felt that in this case the rank and file of the party in the home constituencies had stiffened parliamentary backbones and "within a few days I was surrounded by a party practically united in a firm determination to fight the reciprocity proposals to the bitter end."

When the debate resumed in February 9, Cochrane was in Ottawa. A few days earlier his mother had died in Clarenceville, Quebec, at the age of eighty-eight. He had gone there to handle funeral arrangements, and to arrange care for his father, now ninety-two, who was invited to the homes of his children to live out his life but preferred to stay on the family farm. (He died a few months later.) When Cochrane detoured through Ottawa on his way back to Toronto, he found Borden probing accurately for tender spots in the reciprocity agreement. One was that the policy of the government seemed pointed at free trade with the United States, a complete negation of Canadian policy which for fifty years had spent vast sums on rail and water transportation to bind the nation together from coast to coast. All this would count for little if trade routes suddenly were made to run north and south instead of east and west. Also, Laurier and Fielding said the Commons had to accept this treaty as a whole—and yet it had no definite period of tenure. The slightest alteration could cause complete abrogation of the agreement by the United States at any time, which would hardly cause a ripple in the larger country but could be disaster in Canada. Later that same day the crumbling of the Liberal position began to show. George Foster, his faith apparently renewed, cuttingly analysed the danger that would ensue from the agreement to Canada as an independent nation. Soon after, one of the strongest (however intransigent) Liberals of the time, Clifford Sifton, admitted that Foster's arguments were unanswerable. Less than three weeks later, with the debate still in progress,

Sifton stated his opposition to his own government's plan.

The debate dragged on. Early in May, Laurier gave notice that he would adjourn the Commons to attend an Imperial Conference in London. That night, May 5, Borden gathered all his members and some of the party's main people from the provinces together for dinner. It was a jubilant affair. Cochrane attended with Whitney. The reciprocity debate would be continued when Laurier returned from London in July but already the word was out among the Conservatives to prepare for an election. Then it became apparent that the Tories were going to get some unexpected help from the United States. President Taft made a speech saying that under reciprocity, American farmers would sell more agricultural products to Canada than Canada would sell to the United States. Whitney wired Borden, "Taft's speech . . . should be plastered on every barn and other available spot in the Dominion of Canada."

While Cochrane went about that summer checking Ontario, constituency by constituency, Borden headed west with a war party including eight other prominent Tories. This was reciprocity country; the grain-growers were all for it. But eastern political writers were along. Borden spoke 124 times in 21 days and his uncompomising stand was headlined in all eastern papers as well as in the western ones. In Brandon, when a huge delegation of grain-growers demanded that Borden support reciprocity, he told them that he knew how powerful they were but "if you were able and were prepared to make me prime minister tomorrow on condition that I would support this pact, I would not do it."

One voice rang out from the back: "That's the answer to give!"

And one could almost imagine tens of thousands of Ontario newspaper readers the next day nodding at that cry and saying, "Yes."

When Laurier returned to Parliament July 18, he allowed the debate on this and other matters to resume for ten days. Then he went to see the Governor General, Lord Grey, and announced that Parliament was dissolved for an election to be held September 21. Laurier's statement a day later made it clear that the election would be fought on the reciprocity issue, charging that Tory obstructionism was thwarting the achievement of something the country had always wanted. But even the Liberals were now divided on the issue. Sifton announced he would not run but would campaign against his own party on its reciprocity stand.

Borden's campaign began in London, Ontario, on August 16, with Cochrane on the platform. Cochrane accompanied Borden to speak at many other Ontario points before Borden headed east to Quebec and the Maritimes. Then Cochrane returned to his election headquarters in Toronto. The summer weather was hot and steamy but he was hardly ever in his Rosedale home more than overnight for the next few weeks. Every photo taken of him in that time showed him in a bowler hat, high stiff collar with a small tie nestled at the base, white vest, dark suit, well-shined shoes. But there must have been times when he took off his coat and rolled up his sleeves, because even in the overheated election campaigns of the time there had seldom been one like this.

He made sure that all his candidates on the hustings had the kind of ammunition to appeal to the aroused nationalism, allied with British loyalties, of the crowd. Any speaker rising on any platform had, for instance, a copy of a letter President Taft had written to former President Theodore Roosevelt earlier that year about reciprocity. It was dated January 11, 1911 (coincidentally, the anniversary of Sir John A. Macdonald's birth)—before the plan even had been introduced in the Canadian Commons. And it read:

> It [reciprocity] might at first have a tendency to reduce the cost of food products somewhat; it would certainly make the reservoir much greater and prevent fluctuations. Meantime the amount of Canadian products we would take would produce a current of business between Western Canada and the United States that *would*

> *make Canada only an adjunct of the United States.*
> It would transfer all their important business to Chicago
> and New York, with their bank credits and everything
> else. . . . [Italics added.]

In the same letter he also made a reference to Canada as
being "at a parting of the ways" with her British past. What
could be more effective campaign material among British
loyalists than that? Well, there was one even a little better.
James Beauchamp (Champ) Clark, House leader of the
Democratic party in the U.S. House of Representatives, declared that he favoured reciprocity because

> I hope to see the day when the American flag will
> float over every square foot of the British North Ameri-
> can possession, clear to the North Pole. . . . I have no
> doubt whatever that the day is not far distant when
> Great Britain will joyfully see all her North American
> possessions become part of this Republic. That is the
> way things are tending now. . . .

But from the angry crowds, when these words were read,
would come the roar: "Not by a damn sight!"

One other political grenade of the day was often used to
close off meetings. There is no direct affirmation that Cochrane
had the original idea of using it, although there was some
innuendo in the *Sudbury Journal* one day when it noted: "The
Conservative who dug down into the depths of his memory and
resurrected this old war chant and made it the battle cry in
Ontario for this election, was a wily old fish." Editor Orr, at
least, was crediting—or blaming—his old adversary Cochrane.

It was a verse written twenty years before by a newspaperman in Dundas named R. B. Kernighan. It was published in
every paper, the *Journal* said, recited by every speaker along
the back concessions. And it was called,

THE MEN OF THE NORTHERN ZONE

Oh! We are the men of the Northern Zone.
Shall a bit be placed in our mouth?

If ever a Northerner lost his throne
Did the conqueror come from the South?
Nay! Nay! And the answer blent,
In Chorus is southward sent!
Since when has a Southerner's conquering steel
Hewed out in the north a throne?
Since when has a Southerner placed his heel
On the Men of the Northern Zone?
Our hearts are as free as the rivers that flow
To the seas where the North Star shines,
Our lives are free as the breezes that blow
Through the crests of our native pines.
We never will bend the knee,
We'll always and aye be free,
For liberty reigns in the land of the leal,*
Our brothers are round her throne,
A Southerner never shall place his heel
On the Men of the Northern Zone.

Cochrane toured the North late in August, and spoke at George Gordon's nomination meeting. Early in September Laurier, who already had conceded privately that most of the big Ontario cities were lost, moved into Sudbury. The heavy French-Canadian vote there had been good to him in past elections. The *Journal* called it the greatest political meeting ever held in the Nipissing and Algoma districts. Cochrane must have agreed. He hastily arranged to have the fervent Quebec Nationalist Henri Bourassa brought to Sudbury to help shore up the dikes. Bourassa already had damaged Laurier badly in Quebec, calling him a traitor to the French, a captive of British Ontario. If he helped at all, he helped just enough, in Northern Ontario, because when the election came on September 21 George Gordon's plurality was less than 100 and W. R. Smyth won Algoma with not much more.

When the returns began to come in that night, Laurier in Quebec City and Borden in Halifax sat tensely waiting. Cochrane in Ontario professed not to be quite as tense. He had sent Borden a telegram a week before stating flatly that he

*An archaic Scottish word meaning loyal.

would sweep Ontario and win the country. As he was a careful man about over-statement, he must have meant what he said. Laurier barely held the Maritimes, and Borden felt some moments of doubt. But when the Quebec returns began to come in, his doubt vanished—and so did Laurier's. Laurier's hold on Quebec dropped from 53-11 at dissolution to a tight 37-27 as Conservatives and Bourassa's Nationalists cut in heavily. Ontario results made it official: the Conservatives jumped from 48 seats to 72, and the Liberals faded from 36 to 13.

As the trend became apparent on the bulletin boards outside downtown newspaper offices, the crowds began to celebrate. Throngs estimated by the *Globe* at 150,000 took over the downtown Toronto area bounded by Queen, Church, Front, and York streets. The passions of the campaign were reflected in jubilant, name-calling demonstrations in front of the two Liberal newspapers, the *Globe* and the *Star*—and a brick was thrown through a second-floor window of the *Globe*. (This was still fairly harmless compared to an occurrence at about the same hour in Campbellton, N.B. A Liberal named Dr. Doherty and a Conservative named J. D. Bruce, both respected citizens, argued over the election results. It ended only when Dr. Doherty stabbed Bruce in the eye with his umbrella, and killed him.) Before midnight, the results were nearly complete from the West as well. Alberta and Saskatchewan, the big Reciprocity provinces, had gone to Laurier; but Manitoba and British Columbia had followed the rest of the nation to Borden. A reporter found Premier Whitney and Cochrane together in a victorious gathering of Conservatives at Queen's Park. Premier Whitney repeated the anti-reciprocity sentiments he had spoken many times since the previous winter and said the people apparently agreed. But, reported the *Globe,* "Hon. Frank Cochrane, whose work in charge of the Ontario organization helped materially in the defeat of the government was willing to let bygones be bygones now that it was over. 'Let it rest,' was the only statement he would make."

CHAPTER TEN

A letdown on the day after an election is a condition that exists in any age. When there is no change of government, it is a time for catching up on sleep and preparing to leave on holidays. But when a government with fifteen years' service is toppled, only the newly defeated have real leisure. As soon as the Ontario returns started rolling in, Cochrane knew he'd have another campaign soon, one that he would recommend strongly: an election in Ontario to take advantage of the obvious Conservative popularity. Also, in organizing Ontario for Borden he had lured eight members from the Ontario legislature to run federally. All had won and those seats needed filling—as well as, he must have suspected even then, his own.

Less than thirty-six hours after Borden's triumph was confirmed, the full Ontario cabinet met. That was Saturday morning, September 23, when the leaves were turning to autumn colours on the big trees in Queen's Park. The papers already had forecast an Ontario election, but when Cochrane limped out of the cabinet room with other ministers in early afternoon none would comment. A car was waiting for Cochrane. Only a few colleagues, and his secretary, George Yates, knew precisely where he was heading: a place to fish and play cards and relax, a camp deep in the woods of Algonquin Park.

Borden by that time had travelled from Halifax to his home at Grand Pré, Nova Scotia, for a weekend visit. On Tuesday, September 26, Borden arrived in Ottawa by train to find 20,000 cheering citizens gathered around the station to greet him. The previous day he had written to Cochrane and Whitney.

To Whitney: "I would esteem it a great favor if you would arrive in Ottawa on Wednesday morning as I wish to consult with you concerning some matters of importance and urgency. I have also asked Cochrane to come." Whitney replied by telegram that he was unable to go on Wednesday and ". . . Other man is out of the City for several days . . ." Thursday was decided upon. Whitney to Borden again: "At this moment I cannot tell whether Mr. Cochrane will come down or not. At present his secretary is up at Algonquin Park with a view to giving him your letter and a message from myself."

When Borden's letter to Cochrane had arrived on September 26, George Yates had opened it. "You have helped to let me in for this," was Borden's message for Cochrane, "and now you must help me out."

Yates immediately packed a small bag and started for Algonquin Park. He knew the forestry station that had been Cochrane's take-off point. Yates arrived there in threatening weather which broke furiously into a storm soon after he had set out by canoe accompanied by guides. Reported the *Globe* two days later: "It was a canoe trip of 20 miles through heavy wind and rain, during which the party had several thrilling experiences. When Yates reached his destination deep in the woods with Borden's message Cochrane broke camp immediately and returned to civilization." On September 28 he arrived in Ottawa accompanied by Whitney.

Newspaper headlines read: "Borden Besieged". Applicants for cabinet posts were lined up from sea to sea. Borden was in his Ottawa home, working on plans for his cabinet. Dozens of advocates of this hopeful or that were waiting outside his study and had been for hours. But, reported the *Globe,* there was no delay Thursday evening when Cochrane and Whitney "appeared on the scene to confer with Mr. Borden in regard to the new crew for the Canadian ship of state. They were ushered right in immediately, though others had waited long."

They spent several hours conferring with Borden. Said the *Globe*:

> The Hon. Frank Cochrane shares with Sir James the honor of primary selection. His services in the campaign and the close personal friendship between him and Mr. Borden are responsible for well authenticated reports that he has the choice of four portfolios, all of them most urgent, including those of Public Works, and Railways and Canals.

At the same time Whitney was being offered the Justice ministry. There was an element of haste. The Governor General Earl Grey, who had advised friends in England that Laurier was certain to win the election on the reciprocity issue, rather fortuitously (his leaning to Laurier being so well known) was being replaced. The election upset made him postpone his departure. The new Governor General, the Duke of Connaught, was due to arrive in Quebec on October 13. If Borden were to greet the Duke and Duchess of Connaught as prime minister, accompanied by his new cabinet, a tight schedule had to be met. While Canadian newspapers were still reflecting with amazement on the rout of the Liberals (seven of Laurier's ministers had been defeated, including Fielding, the architect of Reciprocity, and the then much less important W. L. Mackenzie King), Borden was picking and choosing.

On Friday, September 29, reporters stationed at the entrance to Borden's home noted that Whitney and Cochrane arrived again, this time accompanied by Dr. J. D. Reid, the member for Grenville. They were followed into Borden's study a little later by the dour Frederick D. Monk, a Commons veteran and one of the leaders of the anti-British Quebec Nationalists, and by Henri Bourassa, the fiery orator who was the heart of the Nationalists—and who had been imported to Sudbury by

Cochrane to offset Laurier's visit there during the campaign. (This move by Cochrane infuriated the *Toronto Telegram,* whose Tory leanings were not as strong as its imperialism, plus a strong anti-French and anti-Catholic fixation. Because of Cochrane's enlisting of Bourassa's help, the *Telegram* later recommended editorially that the electorate, rather than put Cochrane in the House of Commons, "strangle" him for this infamous alliance.)

After this second conference with Borden, Cochrane and Whitney left Ottawa by Friday overnight train for Toronto. Waiting reporters visiting Whitney in his office Saturday morning were told that he had declined Borden's invitation to join the cabinet. The reporters couldn't question Cochrane. He had gone straight from the train back to Algonquin Park to resume his fishing trip.

Cochrane returned to Toronto the following Tuesday, too late for a cabinet meeting which again broke up with its members silent about an election. Whitney informed his cabinet that day that Cochrane wouldn't be with them much longer. The part that Cochrane was taking in Borden's inner circle was indicated in a telegram he sent October 4 to Borden asking an urgent audience for a visitor from Toronto. On the same morning Borden wired Cochrane, "I would like to see you here tomorrow morning. Can you come?" Cochrane replied, "Yes, will be there."

Borden's cabinet-making difficulties, and occasional references to Cochrane's counsel in these matters, are mentioned in his memoirs. "For many days my house was besieged," he wrote, "and there were excursions and alarums from all parts of the country." In addition to his offer to Sir James Whitney, he had asked Premier Richard McBride of British Columbia to join the cabinet. This was an indication of Borden's nature. A rebellious group in his party had been pushing McBride as new party leader in 1910. Borden knew it, but still had arranged a meeting in Ottawa at which McBride spoke—and didn't impress his listeners, ending that potential threat. However, he felt that McBride's help in the campaign merited a cabinet post if he wanted it. McBride declined. So did Bourassa—he had helped destroy Laurier, but soon would turn on Borden, too, and must have wanted to stay clear of commitments.

In the end, Borden wrote, his principal difficulties were with four persons. George Eulas Foster had been finance minister under John A. Macdonald and wanted to be again.* Borden thought that would be unwise. He didn't say why, but some charges against Foster, never proved, still lingered as a bad taste.

Eventually, Foster "with good grace" took Trade and Commerce. Borden believed the ebullient colonel from Lindsay, Ontario, Sam Hughes, had earned a cabinet post, "but I hesitated for some time because of his erratic temperament, and his immense vanity." Eventually Hughes was given Militia and Defence; a choice that was to add many colourful

---

* At an Ottawa Press Gallery dinner three years later, the members made up a parody of the Parliamentary Guide. This was the "biography" of Foster, in verse:

FOSTER, GEORGE EULAS

It is said he could talk before he could walk,
and his words were never few,
and he'd made a name at the Tempr'ance game,
before his whiskers grew.
So Sir John took him in to tally the tin,
and sit on the Treasury lid,
and he made good there, and everywhere,
and at everything he did.
He could make men cheer, or dribble a tear,
and would wallop the Grits kerflop,
but do what he could and try as he would,
he never got quite to the top.
For as Rufe said slow—one night beflow,
when the boys were having a smile,
"Say, George, old man, you could run dis land,
if you'd licker up once in a while."

and even incredible episodes to Canada's political and military affairs in the next few years.

Robert Rogers, of Manitoba, a noted backroom politician, urgently wanted Railways and Canals, but Borden wrote politely that he didn't think that desirable. Again, the reason was not spelled out but it was mainly because of Rogers' association with persons who had made fortunes out of western land deals resulting from railroad-building grants. Borden offered Rogers the Department of the Interior, "which he eventually accepted, although with considerable reluctance and rather keen disappointment."

"The Department of Railways and Canals I entrusted to Mr. Cochrane," Borden wrote, "whose ability was conceded and who had given yeoman service throughout the campaign." Such as organizing the campaign for the greatest majority the party ever had achieved in Ontario.

Cochrane was also involved in discussions regarding other potential ministers. One was Dr. J. D. Reid, who had been part of a dump-Borden movement in the party three years before, and whose usefulness Borden therefore naturally doubted. But, "Mr. Cochrane was strongly in his favor and begged me to forgive Reid's past disloyalty. Finally I sent for Reid and delivered a rather strong lecture. He promised to . . . be loyal at all times in the future. This pledge he faithfully observed. . . ."

One major battle in which Cochrane took part was over the inclusion of W. Thomas White. He was one of eighteen prominent Toronto Liberals who had left that party over Reciprocity and had campaigned against Laurier, although without seeking election. (Clifford Sifton did the same.) Borden felt that this group deserved representation in the cabinet. Strong arguments from what the *Globe* called "the influential Toronto policy dictators of Conservative policy" were made on White's behalf, but it turned out later the power brokers were badly split on this matter. White was only forty-five, vice-president and general manager of the then fledgling National Trust

Company. On circumstantial evidence, it appears that Cochrane and Whitney supported White's inclusion, because the *Globe* reports of Toronto support closely followed their visit to Ottawa. Also, Whitney mentioned the matter in a letter to a constituent who had protested that Andrew Broder was left out of the cabinet because of capitalist pressure to get White in. "I personally know," Whitney wrote to Irwin Hilliard of Morrisburg, "that it was only with the utmost difficulty that Mr. White was induced to join the government. . . ." But Borden himself wrote that some Toronto Tories were almost fanatically against White. One anti-White messenger Borden refused to receive in his own home but did meet briefly at the front gate. The word was a virtual ultimatum: "Don't appoint White." Borden stiffly replied that he would appoint White, if White would accept. The visit by Cochrane October 5 that Borden had requested apparently helped to settle the White matter. Borden then offered White the Finance portfolio, which he accepted.*

Laurier handed his resignation to Earl Grey at 3 p.m., October 6. Three hours later Borden went to Government House with his still-secret cabinet list, as follows:

Prime Minister and President of the Privy Council	Robert L. Borden
Minister of Trade and Commerce	George Eulas Foster
Minister of the Interior	Robert Rogers
Minister of Public Works	Frederick Debartsch Monk
Minister of Railways and Canals	Francis Cochrane
Minister of Finance	William Thomas White
Postmaster General	Louis Philippe Pelletier
Minister of Marine, Fisheries and Naval Service	John Douglas Hazen

* White served with distinction. When Borden eventually resigned the prime-ministership in 1920, White was an almost unanimous choice of the cabinet as his successor. White declined because of poor health, although a simple yes would have made him prime minister. Arthur Meighen was the second choice.

Minister of Justice	Charles Joseph Doherty
Minister of Militia and Defence	Sam Hughes
Minister of Agriculture	Martin Burrell
Secretary of State	William James Roche
Minister of Labour	Thomas Wilson Crothers
Minister of Inland Revenue and Mines	Wilfrid Bruno Nantel
Minister of Customs	John Dowsley Reid
Ministers Without Portfolio	George Halsey Perley
	Albert Edward Kemp
	James Alexander Lougheed, Senator

According to Borden, the Governor General criticized only one appointment, that of Sam Hughes. That, of course, was private at the time. However, there was no lack of partisan public criticism, with a charge in Liberal papers that it had been Toronto's Bay Street that had refused the Finance portfolio to George Foster, and that Bob Rogers of Manitoba was too much under the wing of Clifford Sifton to do Canada much good. More firmly based was a general conviction that the cabinet might be at serious odds between ministers who had pledged a new naval policy to aid Britain in time of war, and powerful Quebeckers such as Monk who during the campaign had denounced naval participation in any form whatsoever. Less acerbic commentators contented themselves with totting up where the ministers had been born (seven in Quebec, including Cochrane; six in Ontario; two in New Brunswick; Borden in Nova Scotia; Perley in the United States; and Burrell in England) and working out an average age (the middle fifties). Cochrane, at fifty-eight, was in the upper age group and Finance Minister White, at forty-five, was youngest.

The bulk of the cabinet represented ridings in Ontario and Quebec, but each western province was given one position, the first time in Canadian history that western representation had been so high in the cabinet. Roche was from Manitoba (Marquette). Rogers was a Manitoban, but a Saskatchewan seat would be opened for him. Lougheed, government leader in the Senate, was from Alberta. Burrell would represent British Columbia. An interesting point in retrospect is that two men who were in the House, and were to become party leaders and prime ministers, were not considered: Arthur Meighen from Portage la Prairie, and R. B. Bennett from Calgary.

Cochrane left Toronto again for Ottawa on October 9, and at 1.30 that following morning Borden finally made public his cabinet. They were sworn in at noon on October 10. Seven had managed to round up frock coats and silk toppers for the ceremony. The others, including Cochrane, were in business suits. On the following day an order-in-council appointed White, Foster, Doherty, Cochrane, Monk, and Rogers to the powerful Treasury Board, in control of govenment spending.

Cochane and his wife immediately went back to their hotel to pack and leave by special train, with all the other new cabinet members and their wives, for Quebec City to take part in the welcome for the new Governor General. Having been out of power so long, none in the eighteen-man cabinet had experience in pomp and ceremony of this magnitude. None possessed the Windsor ceremonial uniform which was considered *de rigueur* for such occasions (although all were said to have ordered them, at $900 each, to be ready in time for Parliament's opening a month later). When they filed into the crowded Château Frontenac lobby in Quebec just off the train at 11 p.m., October 12, the ministers and their wives were warmly applauded. This welcome put them at ease. Laurier himself, with the rather chivalrous comment, "It is Borden's day," stayed away.

Changing his career at age fifty-eight, even for the larger scene of federal politics, later was said by Cochrane's son Wilbur to have been a reluctant move. While Alice Cochrane enjoyed the pomp and circumstance of the vice-regal welcome in Quebec, a day or two later she was home in Rosedale and Cochrane was at Queen's Park winding up this one part of his life and preparing for the next. "It was a hard decision for him to make," George Yates, the ever-present secretary, wrote in 1950. "He was not at all happy about it."

He didn't have a seat in the Commons. As Ontario organizer, he was in charge of finding seats, not only for himself, but for others such as W. T. White. Of course, the situation wasn't new to Cochrane. It was the second time in just over six years he had been given a major political post without the burden of running for election first. The solution this time was easier than it had been on the Ontario scene in 1905. Cochrane cleaned up his work at Queen's Park and turned his office over to William H. Hearst. It was the agreement they'd made in 1905 coming true. Then he arranged that the Leeds seat in Eastern Ontario would be opened for White. The seventy-one-year-old reeve of Gananoque, George Taylor, had won election to the Commons eight times since 1882, and was ready to go. Cochrane looked around the North for a volunteer to open a seat for himself. He didn't have to look far. His old friend George Gordon resigned the seat he'd just retained in Nipissing. On November 3, Cochrane was nominated, the Liberals refrained from contesting, and Cochrane moved to the Commons as he had originally entered the Ontario legislature, by acclamation.

Meanwhile, both Cochrane and Gordon, like old war-horses, already were working on organization for the December 11 Ontario election called by Whitney. This one wasn't really in doubt. The Liberals, dispirited by the major losses in September, put up only token resistance. They did persuade their leader, Alexander G. MacKay, to resign, and offered the leadership to W. L. Mackenzie King, Laurier's former labour minister who had lost his Waterloo seat in the Borden landslide.

"They offered to provide a salary of $5,000 which in addition to the indemnity of $1,500 would have secured me $6,500 a year," King wrote to a friend a few weeks later. But he declined: he felt the prospects were too meagre. ". . . It might have meant the premiership of Ontario in four years,

but what after all is that?" he observed, in what still stands as
a massive disparagement of provincial politicians. But he did
promise to help Newton W. Rowell, the Toronto lawyer
eventually chosen as Liberal leader. King helped to draft a
platform, helped to campaign, and at the end was fairly well
satisfied when the Liberals gained four seats, from 17 to 21.
"We had really not expected to hold what he had," King
wrote. Cochrane was active in that election, leaving his Commons seat on quick trips by private railway car to speak
throughout the North on behalf of his old flock; helping his
protégé, Charles McCrea, to win Cochrane's former seat in
Sudbury easily, and his successor in Lands and Mines, William
Hearst, to win as easily in Sault Ste. Marie.

While in the North that autumn Cochrane also supervised
the cutting of several business ties. After he entered Whitney's
cabinet in 1905, his hardware company had been managed by
others and in 1909 had been converted into a joint stock
company still with family control. Also, he and William Mc-
Vittie—still his partner in the Wahnapitae Power Company—
owned the north half of Lot 7 in the 6th concession of McKim
Township. That may not sound like much until one learns that
it was on the other (south) half of Lot 7 that Thomas Frood
had made his great mineral discovery in 1884. The world's
nickel market then was controlled by two great companies,
International Nickel and Mond. Both had properties and
smelters in the Sudbury area. In 1911 Cochrane completed
sale to Mond of the property he and McVittie held, by then
called the Frood Extension. Cochrane's share was not much
more than $100,000, for what within a few years was valued
at many millions.

On November 15, when the Throne Speech for the new
session was read by the Duke of Connaught in the House of
Commons, Cochrane was in his seat.

His direct ties with the government of Ontario were fully
unravelled although he continued to be Whitney's voice with
Borden. His home was still in Toronto, with a hotel room in

Ottawa while an apartment was made ready. But now he was fully settled into his office in the West Block, with its vast view of the Upper Ottawa and the Gatineau Hills, getting acquainted with the immensities of his new department.

CHAPTER ELEVEN

In assessing Cochrane's performance in the Commons during his first session, one impression emerges instantly: no minister in the House faced such knowledgeable and resourceful adversaries. A major preoccupation of the nation for more than three decades had been railroad-building, and many times it had been a subject of political fire and fury in the House of Commons. For fifteen years the Liberals had been defending their railroad policies against Conservative charges of bungling, waste, and extravagance. Now it was their turn to snipe where they could—and also to defend their own records when in office. This was not always easy. Sir Wilfrid Laurier in 1904 had estimated that the total cost to the government of the National Transcontinental Railway, then about to be built under a complicated deal with the Grand Trunk, would be not a cent more than $13 million. Cochrane's current estimate of cost was around $187 million, with completion estimates beyond that. One of Borden's campaign promises had been for a full investigation of the National Transcontinental.*

* Soon after the election, the Hon. S. N. Parent, Laurier's appointee as president of National Transcontinental Commission, resigned and was replaced by R. W. Leonard, who had held many important railroad and hydro appointments earlier.

That put Laurier in the forefront of many debates over railways, defending former policies and attacking new ones. Often when Laurier got in on one side, Borden would come in to support Cochrane on the other. Another Liberal attacker was Henry R. Emmerson, who had been Minister of Railways and Canals from 1904 to 1907. He was an incisive debater but had a rich reputation for hitting the bottle. Laurier had almost fired him after one 1906 escapade, but relented to the extent that he left Emmerson in office after writing out a declaration, and getting Emmerson to sign it. It read:

> I hereby pledge my word to Sir Wilfrid Laurier that I never will again taste wine, beer or any other mixed or intoxicating liquor, in token of which I place in Sir W. L.'s hands my resignation as a member of the cabinet and Minister of Railways with the date in blank, leaving it to him to fill in the blank and act upon it should I fail my promise.
>
> Henry R. Emmerson.

In 1907, the time had come to fill in the blank date. Emmerson's indiscretions had figured in a scathing attack by Bourassa on wrong-doers of both federal parties. Emmerson left the cabinet, with a short gem of a Commons speech for posterity, on April 2, 1907: "I have never been, mark my words, Mr. Speaker," he said, "and I make them with the full knowledge of the solemnity of the occasion and the dignity of my position —I have never been in a hotel in Montreal with a woman of ill repute."

But the punishment partially reformed him, and four years later he was a formidable member of the forces attacking the new minister, Cochrane.

A third telling critic was Cochrane's immediate predecessor in Railways and Canals, the ambitious, fair, and able Brockville editor, George Graham. He had been beaten in the general election but was the first of Laurier's old ministers to get back into the House. This he did in a South Renfrew by-election in February 1912, adding his expertise to the array of Cochrane's formidably well-grounded antagonists. Not many new ministers in major portfolios are faced with two former ministers and a prime minister, all with greater first-hand knowledge of the subject than the new man could be expected to have.*

But this situation proved valuable in the long run to Cochrane. The overwhelming nature of the attack helped establish his own uncompromising personality. He refused to dissemble. If he didn't know the answer to a question—and often he didn't, as they came literally by the hundreds while the House sat from November 15 to December 7 and then resumed January 10—he simply said so.

When he said once to a question, "I do not know," his questioner demanded, "Who is going to know if the Minister does not?"

Cochrane replied quietly, "Do you want me to make up a story? I do not know."

Upon taking office he immediately stopped certain controversial programs that were under way—including construction of a railway terminal in Quebec City, and a contract the Laurier government had awarded a few months earlier to begin work on the Hudson Bay Railway—while he had his own assessments made of what policy should be. When there was doubt in himself or among his officials, he simply called a recess before deciding to carry on with the previous govern-

* Another virulent attacker was F. B. (Fighting Frank) Carvell of New Brunswick. The Press Gallery's burlesque edition of the Parliamentary Guide saw him this way:

CARVELL, FRANKIE: A semi-mythical personage, believed by many to be the reincarnation of the gentleman who cut off Lady Jane Grey's head. The name is obviously a corruption of Carve well. Elected official executioner of the Liberal party in 1904, and is noted for the genial way in which he performs his gruesome duties. Lifelong abstainer from all intoxicants except human blood.

ment's policy, replacing it with one of his own, or killing it altogether (as sometimes happened).

One minor example of his style in the House came after he ordered work stopped on the Holland River branch of the Trent Canal, a $2 million project. One of his ministerial predecessors, Emmerson, questioned this stoppage. Another, Graham, took it up, saying there was a great need for the canal in the Newmarket and Aurora areas.

Graham mentioned that petitions were being circulated to have the work re-started. "As a matter of fact, at the inception of this canal," Graham intoned, "Grits, Tories and all others in that part of the country were very enthusiastic for it."

Cochrane replied tersely, "To get the money spent," and would not budge, his idea being that one could get up a petition anywhere in favour of the government's spending money.

No cabinet minutes were kept at that time in a form that may be consulted now, so there is no on-the-spot record of his views on matters that did not touch on his department or his role as the clearing-house for Ontario appointments. A major political issue for years had been naval policy: how Canada would support Britain at sea (if at all) in time of war. Laurier had passed his naval bill in 1910—in effect, to set up a Canadian navy. Two old cruisers, the *Rainbow* and the *Niobe*, had been bought as training ships, but little else had been done. During the campaign, Borden had criticized the Laurier naval policy, saying it would create a force "that will be absolutely useless in time of war and therefore of no practical benefit to Canada or to the Empire. It will cost immense sums of money to build, equip and maintain. It will probably result in time of war in the useless sacrifice of many valuable lives, and it will not add one iota to the fighting strength of the Empire. The more it is considered, the more does it become evident that the whole naval plan of the government is an unfortunate blunder."

Still, as Laurier knew, Borden's eventual course would be simply another form of naval force but one more directly committed to support Britain. Laurier knew that many of Borden's Quebec supporters wanted no naval policy of any kind and that pressures from English Canada which had forced Laurier into his original naval policy would be felt again by Borden.

When Laurier listened to the Duke of Connaught read the Throne Speech on November 15 and it contained no mention at all of naval policy, he shrewdly brought this split in Borden's ranks into the open immediately. He expressed surprise that no mention of naval policy had been made and, in a course then unprecedented, moved that the makeup of the cabinet "should not receive the approval of the House". He argued that "there is in the present cabinet a flagrant conflict of opinion [in] that some of its members have repeatedly, both before and during the last elections, denounced naval defence in any form whatsoever."

Borden replied that liberty of opinion was allowed to the representatives of the people—even when these opinions disagreed. He didn't give an inch in the ensuing debate on the Throne Speech, and eventually after a debate of two weeks Laurier's anti-cabinet amendment was voted down and the Throne Speech passed.

A sidelight to these early weeks was a matter that still could happen in some form today. Borden had chosen as Speaker an elderly Western Ontario member (since 1878), Dr. T. S. Sproule. He was also a leading Orangeman. It was the custom that prayers were read in English and French on alternate days. Dr. Sproule did not speak French but, a conscientious man, arrived in Ottawa weeks before the House opened and took French instruction. On his first attempt to read the prayers in French, using his new-found training backed up by a phonetic card, Sproule did reasonably well. But Borden, Cochrane, and others chuckled over an exchange that day between two desk-mates on the new government's front bench. Thomas White and F. D. Monk, the Quebec leader, sat together. At the end of Sproule's limping

French prayers White leaned over and said, "That was very good, was it not, Monk?"

Monk (in a deep and rather sepulchral voice) : "I have no doubt that Almighty God would understand it."

Every question period during these early days found Cochrane bombarded by Liberal questions about dismissals from government railway and canal jobs, which always had been considered patronage appointments. When Laurier took power in 1896 there were wholesale dismissals of Conservatives so that Liberals could replace them. (Commons returns gave long lists of such dismissals.) Many of these Conservatives, fifteen years later, wanted their jobs back. Cochrane's own colleagues pressed him for such action, but he had ruled (an extension of his earlier Ontario policy) that a man could be dismissed only for cause, including proof of partisan political activity—campaigning, making up voters lists, fund-raising, etc. Even while pressing the questions, Liberals frequently admitted his fairness. On one occasion one such questioner, Charles A. Gauvreau (Liberal, Temiscouata), having received his answer from Cochrane, remarked: "I am quite ready to thank the minister for what he has done. He has practically refused the request of certain partisans to make a clean sweep of [Liberal appointees among] Intercolonial Railway employees, and he has been manly enough not to dismiss anybody without granting an investigation. That is the difference between him and some of his colleagues. He has even gone so far as to return to their jobs some men who had been dismissed, and I thank him for that."

The first Throne Speech in the Borden regime mentioned that trade conditions were satisfactory, and the harvest good, and touched other points before coming to what was to become Cochrane's first major test in the Commons, a bill providing for co-operation with the provinces in improving highways.

When in opposition, the Conservatives had argued that the great age of railroad-building was almost over. The next pressing priority, they said, would be to provide for the public a highways network to meet the new growth of automobile traffic. Highways were provincial matters under the British North America Act, but some provinces were financially more able than others to build roads. The government's thinking was that just as federal subsidies had been provided to railroad companies to build railways, money should be made available to the provinces to build and improve specific highways, some provincial and others with interprovincial importance. It was the first attempt at conditional grants to provinces.

This was a popular proposal, especially with the poorer provinces, but it had some built-in difficulties. Some Liberals saw it as another gift to Ontario, which would get the largest grant. Another difficulty was lack of time for discussion with the provinces to work out details. This showed in Cochrane's introduction as he said: "This bill is . . . perhaps a little meagre, but this is because it has been impossible to decide in detail just what is the best way of carrying out the plan proposed. So we propose doing it largely by order-in-council until we get more definite information. The money will be decided the same as our subsidies for different provinces, and the object will be to work with local governments. . . ."

Immediately the crunch came, although only briefly at the first-reading stage.

Laurier asked, "Is this [the division of money] based on population?"

Cochrane: "Yes. I explained that it was to be on the same basis as that upon which [other] subsidies are granted to the provinces."

But this had not been written into the bill. When Cochrane moved second reading (approval in principle) five weeks later, there was some preliminary skirmishing as to where the bill stood under the British North America Act, with Laurier holding that it contravened the Act and Borden arguing that it didn't. Eventually the debate progressed to Laurier's chief objection: "That any appropriations for this purpose can be devoted to two or three provinces, according as the ministry of the day may determine." He demanded that the division-by-population specification that had been mentioned by Cochrane be written into the bill, instead of just being accepted as the spirit of the bill. Obviously, he was afraid that such funds would be used as election pump-priming. Once this line of attack surfaced, it became a favourite of subsequent Liberal speakers. They charged the bill would be no more than a mighty pork barrel. Speakers for the Conservative side argued with equal fervour on Cochrane's behalf that the bill's requirement that each province approve each specific expenditure was a safeguard against any federal electioneering by road contract.

Cochrane contended, with some validity, that his refusal to write the division-by-population clause into the bill, in accordance with his verbal assurance, had a fair and logical basis. He felt that there might be years when a province with a small population but a large geographical area would require a larger per-capita subsidy for roads than would a province with a much larger, but more concentrated, population. Also, he argued, if division-by-population were made the letter of the law, instead of the spirit, and a single province were hit by some natural disaster that made major road-building programs essential, swift action would be difficult without all other provinces—with needs not so urgent—getting money they might not require.

The debate really ran, off and on, for more than two years. Laurier's amendments always could be voted down, and were. But each time the bill passed in the House, with the Liberal amendments defeated, the real roadblock was just ahead: the Senate. After so many years of Liberal governments, the Senate was massively Liberal. It could not kill the bill but could (and did) promptly incorporate into it the same Liberal amendments that the Commons had just voted down. Naturally, on being returned for Commons approval, the bill would be found unacceptable, causing it to be put over to the next session for presentation again; and so on *ad infinitum*.

Borden accused Laurier of instructing his Senators to obstruct the elected body in this way, which Laurier denied. It is unlikely that the Senate needed any instruction. It followed the Commons debates. The highways bill wasn't the only one that suffered. One spirited attack was made by George Foster on Laurier and his Senate leader, former Ontario Liberal Premier George Ross. Foster charged that the Liberals used their partisan majority in the Senate for the purpose of obstructing the goverment and "slaughtering" measures that were wanted by the electorate that had put the Conservatives into power.*

Another Conservative election promise thwarted in this way was one to establish a commission to make a continuing study of the tariff structure so that it would give the maximum benefit in maintaining Canadian industry, full employment, and fair prices. It passed the Commons as the highways bill had, but also was amended in the Senate to make it unacceptable to the government when returned to the Commons. Borden didn't much mind losing the tariff measure, apparently. Finance Minister White had piloted it through the Commons but when it was rejected by the Senate he told Borden he could do without it. It had been a Borden campaign promise at a time when White was still a Liberal. The bill was never introduced again. Cochrane persisted one more year with the highways bill but when it again was rejected by the Liberal Senate he let it drop.

One other instance, a matter dear to Cochrane's heart—

* This was taken into account in the Press Gallery's burlesque biography of Borden in 1914, which went as follows:

BORDEN, ROBERT LAIRD: Cabinet maker in basswood. Refused to annex the United States. Never looks for trouble, doesn't have to. Delivered Canada from the Tuppers to Bob Rogers. Essay: "How I Monkeyed Monk." Promoted amalgamation of Orange Order and Nationalists. Now combining Manufacturers' Association with Grain Growers. Favorite book "Job." War Cry: "Let me finish Laurier's work of reforming the Senate."

even more so than the highways bill—was passed by Commons and then scuppered by the Senate. This was a bill to provide assistance—really a retroactive subsidy—to the Temiskaming and Northern Ontario Railway. Or, as one sharp-tongued Liberal Maritimer, E. M. Macdonald (Pictou), called it, "An Act to provide for giving the province of Ontario a gift of $2,000,000".

Cochrane's railroad subsidies usually went through in batches of many dozens at a time. The committee-stage consideration of subsidies was much less formal, and normally much less combative, than debates on other matters—maybe because the Commons members saw so many railway subsidies pass before their eyes each year. Cochrane would announce something like: "The first 22 resolutions are re-votes," and everyone, shuffling papers, would nod. Then sometimes a local member would make an interjection on behalf of, or opposing, a sub-sidy—describing the route to be served, and dwelling on its value or lack of value. Or sometimes it wouldn't be the local member.

An example, chosen at random, March 22, 1912: The subsidy under consideration was the Ha Ha Bay Railway, mostly for a series of short branch lines.

> Sir Wilfrid: Was there not a change in the route?
> Cochrane: The route was okayed down to the wharf.
> Laurier: It was to pass through the village of La
> Terrière.

He asked that the item be held over pending more informa-tion.

This is given as being typical of the low-keyed and almost gossipy nature in most consideration of railway subsidies. They weren't giving the money away on the spot. Performances had to be met; sometimes payments would be made at the end of a contract, or sometimes at completion of each segment of 10 miles or by other arrangements.

Often Graham and Cochrane made brief comments which

were substantially in agreement. There was also a certain amount of kidding, as when Liberal Frank Oliver, of Edmonton, once asked about a new 100-mile stretch of the Vancouver, Westminster, and Yukon: "Does the 100 miles ... bring construction to any particular important geographical points?"

H. R. Stevens (Liberal, Vancouver): "Not necessarily although it will open up a good piece of territory."

Cochrane, looking realistically into the future: "I am afraid they will be back for more."

Sometimes railways, having received promises of subsidies, then went out and used the promises as collateral in seeking financial support for actual construction. If they didn't get this financing, they might keep having the subsidy re-voted until it finally was forfeited, or some other more active group applied for a subsidy to try the same route. There was curiosity, sometimes, about who owned the railroad company. Cochrane would answer with the names of individuals, or that one of the major lines, such as the C.P.R., owned it. If he had other information, he gave it.

Bruce Mines and Algoma Railway; Calgary and Fernie; Canada and Gulf Terminal; Cariboo, Barkerville, and Willow River; Albert Mines; Kootenay Central; Lac Seul, Rat Portage, and Keewatin; Lake Erie and Northern; Manitoba and Northwestern; St. Charles and Huron; Tillsonburg, Lake Erie, and Pacific—the names rolled on and on, the brief comments were exchanged. It seemed almost somnolent, as if the normal political instincts for the battle had been suspended. And then came the Temiskaming and Northern Ontario, owned then as now by the Province of Ontario, and the attitude changed.

The difference here was that the T. and N. O. was already built, and in operation from North Bay to Cochrane, 252.8 miles. There was some irony in that when the line was started under George Ross's Ontario Liberal government in 1902, Ross applied for a subsidy and Laurier turned him down. Laurier had refused a subsidy again when Whitney's government applied a few years later. But now the federal government was Conservative, and the Ontario government was Conservative. Added to this, Whitney was a very straight-ahead political person; he had helped Borden to win the election and expected certain favours in return. During Cochrane's first session in the Commons he was bombarded with letters from Whitney strictly in the line of: "You're our man in Ottawa." The T. and N.O. subsidy was the first of these demands. On November 15, 1911, the day of the Throne Speech, Whitney wrote two private letters to Cochrane. One was rather breath-taking. Whitney simply asked that Cochrane arrange an adjournment of the Commons from November 30 for two weeks to "give an opportunity for the Ontario members to step in and help us in the [Ontario] elections. . . . I need not say anything as to what the Ottawa people should be ready to do for us."

His second letter that day read:

> I think Matheson [provincial treasurer] will be able to send you today a memorandum relating to our demand for the subsidy for the T. & N.O. Railway. You will observe that he puts the subsidy for the main line at $12,000. per mile in pursuance of the precedent formed when the last Conservative Government made a grant to the C.P.R. and which is explained in the memorandum. You will observe also the reason given for that grant was that it was a connecting link with the Pacific Ocean. Our line has still a strong claim from that point of view, as you know, because it connects Toronto with the Grand Trunk Pacific Railway and makes complete the line across the Continent. I know, of course, that you will do all you can for us in the matter. Of course, if you cannot succeed as to the $12,000. per mile we must be contented with the best you can do. However, I repeat that our claim is good for the larger sum.

The matter was discussed in other letters before Cochrane, January 4, told Whitney, "the subsidy will be granted."

In Cochrane's supporting statement that opened this debate, he was obviously on home ground and his underlying principles showed. "The line was intended to open up the great clay belt in Northern Ontario, of which so much has been heard in the press," he said with the enthusiasm he always felt for the North. "There are claimed to be something in the neighbourhood of 20 million acres of good fertile land capable of raising as good wheat, and especially fall wheat, as [that grown in] the provinces of Manitoba and Saskatchewan. The line . . . has opened up that part of Northern Ontario to development, and has been of great benefit in connection with the building of the Transcontinental Line, enabling supplies to be brought in which otherwise it would have been impossible to transport except in winter by a haul of some 250 miles. . . . It also enables the branch of the Grand Trunk from Toronto to North Bay to connect with the Transcontinental at Cochrane. . . ."

He went on to say how the branch line to Cobalt had enabled low-grade mines to be worked at a profit for the national good; and the branch to Porcupine helped "two or three as good gold mines as are to be found anywhere in the world." The railway therefore had facilitated the development not only of agricultural and lumbering interests, but also the great mining industry in Northern Ontario. Any province that undertook to develop its resources in that way, he argued, ought to receive assistance.

The main thrust of the Liberal attack was that the subsidy was purely political; that subsidies were meant to aid construction, not to bonus lines that already were constructed and operating at a profit. (Cochrane denied that the line was profitable, and later produced figures to back this up.)

One Maritime Liberal said there was no reason why the Dominion government should "contribute $2,000,000 to the exchequer of the province of Ontario unless it be that my hon. friend [Cochrane] wishes to remember his former friends. . . ." Another suggested with a straight face that Ontario had earned the bonus simply by returning so many Conservatives to Parliament in the last election. Laurier attacked (although fairly mildly) the principle that federal money should be given to any railroad owned by a province. Cochrane produced a precedent from 1884 in Quebec, in which Laurier had voted for subsidizing a provincially owned railroad. Laurier retorted that by the time he had done so the road was part of the C.P.R., and therefore a national railroad. He said shrewdly that if Cochrane would declare the T. and N.O. to be a national utility removed from Ontario control, he would vote for the subsidy. This was an admission that Cochrane tucked away for future reference.

The debate ranged on throughout a day before the subsidy was passed. When George Ross's Liberals in the Senate amended it to state that all other provincially built roads that now had become part of national systems should be subsidized retroactively the same way, the Commons refused to agree to the amended act, and so it died.

A year later Cochrane brought it in again. This time he had more ammunition. Part of the Liberal thrust had been that the T. and N.O. was making money. Cochrane was able to show that while there was an operating surplus of revenue over expenditure of about $325,000, fixed-interest charges on bonds amounted to $746,000 annually, leaving a deficit of $423,247. A deal with the Grand Trunk Pacific for running rights reduced this deficit by about $300,000.

He mentioned that the Senate had effectively stalled the bill the previous year but at the same time had approved a larger subsidy for the Canadian Northern in British Columbia ($12,000 a mile versus the $6,400 a mile asked for the T. and N.O.). There were Opposition arguments that the Canadian Northern subsidy was for construction, but Cochrane argued that it was still controlled by British Columbia. In the end, the bill was passed again, and this time Cochrane had figured out the key to getting it past the Senate. This was Laurier's earlier statement that as long as the railroad was purely a provincial matter, he would oppose the subsidy; but if it would submit to federal control in rates for freight that was passed from the T. and N.O. to other carriers, he would not.

On November 5, 1912, in a letter to J. L. Englehart, head of the T. and N.O., Cochrane said he was about to bring the subsidy up again, and would there be any objections to freight leaving the T. and N.O. being billed at rates set by the Dominion Railway Board? "It seems to me that $2,000,000 is a nice thing for any railway to get hold of, and I would be glad to have your opinion on this suggestion." Englehart replied that he had no objection. Early in 1913, the bill passed the Senate with that revision. Cochrane then wrote to Whitney that the Senate had allowed the subsidy, but he urged that it not be applied for until later in the year, because Finance Minister White was facing heavy expenditures and did not wish to borrow at this time.

The pressure put on Cochrane over the T. and N.O. subsidy was only one item in Whitney's flow of requests, demands, advice, and reflections to his former minister during that first winter. On November 17, 1911, he complained that the Throne Speech had not mentioned aid for immigration to New Ontario, and requested an explanation. Cochrane said no mention in the Throne Speech was necessary.

A long-smouldering dispute between Ontario and Manitoba over a new boundary, with Manitoba pressing for a provincial coastline on Hudson Bay, was raised because Whitney thought the Manitoba politicians were asking too much. Ontario wanted to extend the T. and N.O. to a Hudson Bay port. "But of course I feel that you will be watching the situation," Whitney told Cochrane. On November 20, Whitney sent Cochrane a map showing what Ontario felt it must get— a boundary on the Churchill River. He had discussed the boundary with Manitoba government people as far back as 1905 and now charged bad faith on the part of the Manitobans. Cochrane replied mildly with an outline of the situation, saying he was "at a loss to see where there had been bad faith".

Whitney was angered by Cochrane's attitude. On January 24 there was a peremptory tone to a telegram Whitney sent asking Cochrane to Toronto "to consider and discuss fully appropriations for roads as well as the boundary matter". A following letter said the position Cochrane had put forward in cabinet earlier as being Ontario's boundary claims should be considered as "withdrawn until you see us". The final four words were underlined.

Another letter (before the date of Cochrane's conference visit had been decided) mentioned a new boundary proposal which would give Ontario a corridor of land to Hudson Bay, but the proposal "must be kept between Mr. Borden and yourself without being submitted to your colleagues." The weekend meeting that Whitney requested had a quick result: a handwritten note from Cochrane a few days later enclosing a draft order-in-council on the boundary matter, saying "You change this if you do not like the wording of it." A month later Ontario had the concessions it was seeking, which would allow the T. and N.O. access to a port on Hudson Bay, either at Nelson or at Churchill, if it ever decided to use it. (In the late 1920s, the Liberals claimed publicly that Cochrane, as the responsible minister, in 1912 chose Port Nelson as the terminus for the Hudson Bay Railway because it suited the purposes of the T. and N.O. This charge was made years after Cochrane's death, but Borden, in retirement, wrote a letter to R. B. Bennett denying that political reasons had influenced Cochrane's choice of Port Nelson—a choice that the Liberals in the end changed to Churchill anyway.)

The Ontario power-broker role assigned to Cochrane by Whitney was not unusual in politics except perhaps in its intensity. Each part of the country had its power-broker in Ottawa. There was a certain amount of "I'll back your man this time, and you back mine the next" interplay between these ministers on Senate, judicial, and other appointments. For anything going in Ontario, Cochrane had the strongest voice, a result not only of Whitney's support, but also of

Borden's knowledge that Cochrane, who remained as his Ontario chief organizer, had needs of his own in retaining and reinforcing the faithful who won elections.

Despite the imperative nature of some of Whitney's demands during the winter when dozens of letters and telegrams flowed between them, it was March before Cochrane got his back up. This started innocently enough on March 1 when Cochrane wrote Whitney a letter marked "confidential and private" regarding the establishment of an appointment for a junior judge in Lincoln county, which Whitney had been urging, and proposed to cover by Ontario legislation.

Cochrane said he had discussed the matter with Justice Minister Doherty, who felt "that the appointment of County Judges has in the past been more or less of a farce; that it is impossible to get proper men to accept the office on account of the small renumeration, and he feels that if fewer were appointed and the territory enlarged we would get better men and it would be better for the public as a whole."

Cochrane wrote, "You know I hate to oppose anything that you and Mr. [Attorney General J. J.] Foy advocate, because I know you do it with the best intention, but I really concur in Mr. Doherty's view that we have too many County judges, and it seems to me that if any policy could be adopted whereby more efficient men could be got for the Bench it would be much better.

"Mr. Doherty says that he has enquired from some of the legal men there [in Lincoln] and they say that any young man would have no trouble in handling the work in Lincoln; that the present occupant of the Bench is unwell now, but that a Deputy could be appointed whose commission would expire with the retirement or death of the present incumbent. Whereas if a junior judge is appointed now, a junior judge would forever be considered necessary.

"I hope you will not think I am putting my nose in where I have no business, but I am thoroughly in accord with the Minister of Justice's attitude in this matter."

Whitney was so annoyed by Cochrane's position that he drafted a long and hot letter (which he did not mail). He reconsidered for a few days before shortening the letter somewhat and sending it, on March 5:

All this means that the opinion of Mr. Doherty, fortified by inquiries which he has made of people in the locality some at least of whom are interested people, is of a higher value and should be considered instead of the considered action of the Legislature of Ontario under the guidance of the Government. It means that, or it has no meaning. . . .

It may or may not be a fact that there are too many County Judges. This is a matter to be dealt with by the Legislature and not by the Minister of Justice. But if there are, it does not follow that there are too many in the county of Lincoln. Nor does it follow at all that under any new system that might be adopted two judges would still be necessary in Lincoln.

My colleagues and I trust that we have done with argument on this subject. . . . It is my wish that you show this letter to Mr. Borden and Mr. Doherty.

From Cochrane, March 7:

Dear Sir James:

My letter was not intended by me to be an argument. . . .

It was a purely personal letter in which I evidently made the mistake of presuming that our relations have been such that I could pass on, for your information at least, the views of the Minister of Justice in this particular. Your reply has unpleasantly impressed me with the fact that I should let provincial matters severely alone, unless my opinion is invited, and I am somewhat surprised that you should ask me to show such a letter to Mr. Borden or Mr. Doherty. Of course I shall not do any such thing.

From Whitney, March 8:

Dear Cochrane,

I have your letter. It seems I forgot that you have full privilege to write me on any subject saying anything you

choose, while I have no right to say anything that occurs
to me in reply. I have no comment to make on what you
express as being your intention in the future. I will take
my own way of bringing to Mr. Borden's notice what
I stated in my letter to you. It is not of great consequence whether it gets to the knowledge of Mr. Doherty
or not.

For a while, letters between the two were shorter and
cooler, but then normal friendly relations seemed to prevail
once more.

But Cochrane's life wasn't all politics, big and small. A
lot of his letters were from ordinary people who looked to him
for answers to tiny problems. One written March 11, 1912, was
from Mrs. George Mitchell of Cobalt. There were no dairies in
the area and she had bought a Jersey cow. While being taken
to pasture one day, the cow strayed into slag from the nearby
smelter. The slag contained cyanide and the cow died. Mrs.
Mitchell combined a complaint on this matter with a request
for some advice on parliamentary procedure in running the
meetings of a local women's club.

On March 14, Cochrane replied:

Dear Mrs. Mitchell,
    I have your letter of March 11th informing me of the
untimely end of your beloved cow. In this you have my
warm sympathy as I too have experienced the condensed
variety of milk in that north country.
    I note what you say in reference to the rules for
Parliamentary procedure, and I am forwarding under
separate cover the rules of the House of Commons which
I hope will be of some use to you. I would particularly
call your attention to section 21, subsection 1, which says
that no Member may speak twice to a question. I hope
that you and your lady friends will not find this too great
a handicap in debating Ladies Aid matters.
    I shall be very glad indeed if, sometime when I am in
Cobalt, it is possible to call and have dinner.

Very truly yours,
F. Cochrane

CHAPTER TWELVE

An illuminating sidelight on the character of Hon. Frank Cochrane, Minister of Railways and Canals, is revealed in the announcement that he will make his forthcoming trip of inspection of work on the Hudson Bay Railway without the usual corps of ministerial attendants. The minister will make most of the journey in an ordinary canoe with only an Indian guide, and will do his share of the paddling, pitching of tents, making of fires and cooking of meals during the 10 days journey. He will be met at Fort Nelson on Hudson Bay by the Government steamer Stanley.

Sudbury Journal, early July, 1912

The headline on that story read: "Mr. Cochrane will use his own paddle." It wasn't quite that low-budget a journey, in the end. There were three canoes, each manned by three Indian guides. Also he took his Chief Engineer, H. A. Bowden, and his indefatigable secretary, George Yates, who is shown in photos of the trip as erect, short, and dark, a birdlike man, with a neat dark beard, pointed moustaches, and a cap set straight on his head. In pictures of shore activity along the route the nine guides are loading or unloading the canoes, pitching or striking tents. But in all photos showing the little fleet on the water, Cochrane is wielding a paddle. His position was second from the stern, and he stands out distinctively in dozens of photos taken by Yates because on the trail he wore a wide-brimmed felt hat with a white band.

But it would have been quite in keeping with the wildly improbable history of the Hudson Bay Railway if the minister had gone it alone. Or with Yates, on a raft. This project had been chartered to many companies, from 1880 on, and had been a political medicine ball ever since. By 1884 no fewer than nine companies had been chartered to build railways to Hudson Bay. One plan was a direct line from San Francisco to Churchill! Another was a winding 1,600-mile route through the Barren Lands, designed to open up the tundra (for what, nobody was sure).

As unlikely as the Hudson Bay Railway project looked to many, and still does, it had that one majestic requisite for survival in Canada of the time: it could pull western votes and was doing so in Manitoba even before Louis Riel was hanged in 1885. John A. Macdonald used it first. Donald Mann and William Mackenzie, two of the cleverest railroad promoters of the time, were involved at various stages. Liberals later won elections in the new provinces of Alberta and Saskatchewan with the help of Frank Oliver's campaign cry that Laurier was committed to build the Hudson Bay road.

Laurier never apparently liked the idea much but he didn't contradict those of his western organizers who said he did. Just before the 1908 general election, Laurier had pledged his party to immediate construction of the Hudson Bay route and sent out survey parties a few weeks before the polling date as a show of intent.

Even that became a sort of comedy. Chief Government Engineer John Armstrong was to judge between two terminals: Churchill or the closer (by 85 miles) Port Nelson. Churchill had a good small harbour, Port Nelson was a shallow question-mark of shifting silt and channels. But while Armstrong was pondering, he heard that one of Laurier's ministers and his friends had blanketed the approaches to Churchill with land options, in hopes of making big profits. At least partly because of anger at this profiteering attempt, Armstrong chose Port Nelson.

When the 1908 election was won by Laurier, little else was done to fulfill the promise of "immediate construction". Then in the 1911 election Laurier had Reciprocity as his big issue, especially in the west. He didn't think he needed the Hudson Bay plank, so he more or less ignored it on the platform. Cochrane and his colleagues in the Conservative policy committee gratefully snapped it up. G. R. Stevens, in his fascinating history of the Canadian National Railways, wrote: "One of the more astute moves of the Conservatives in the 1911 election was their whole-hearted adoption of the Hudson Bay project. The Tories decked out this foster child in its Sunday Best and paraded it at a thousand whistle-stops in Western Canada as their very own flesh and blood." They knew they needed something in the west to counteract the pull of Laurier's Reciprocity policy there. This was it. They promised to complete the railway "without a single day's unnecessary delay". Even while opposing Reciprocity, the Hudson Bay promise helped them win half the seats in the west, to go with their big gains in Ontario and Quebec.

Due to this campaign promise, one of Cochrane's first moves in his new portfolio was to pull out the departmental files on the Hudson Bay Railway. Wrote Stevens: "There the revelations of unwarranted assumptions and guesswork calculations so shocked him that he halted work pending a reappraisal of the project." But the Hudson Bay route, faulty or not, had an emotional pull Cochrane had underestimated. Western members of both parties swarmed to the attack. In the face of the uproar in his own caucus Borden overruled Cochrane and privately, in cabinet, told him that construction must be resumed soon.

On December 4, 1911, in one of his first debates in the Commons, Cochrane rose to answer the western critics in a comprehensive speech stating that "though my constituency is a long way from Hudson Bay, I believe that the undertaking is in the interests of the whole country." It was his duty to be sure that the details of the project were sound, but "there will be no more delay in the building of that road than is absolutely necessary in the public interest," he said. Laurier entered the debate deploring the delay. Borden countered by saying that the Liberals had promised to have the line operating by then, and that Laurier therefore was urging upon Cochrane "an example that he himself did not follow".

Another lengthy debate followed in January, with the westerners once again in full cry, and this time Cochrane indicated the pressure that had been on him. Aiming his remarks straight at Laurier, he said the meagreness of the information available had astonished him. "Were it not that the route had been surveyed, and the road located, and the contract let, I would not, with the information now before me, consider that the location was the best one. But . . . I find it is now too late to alter it. I have therefore ordered the contractors to proceed." However, the first section was a long way from the sea yet and he still felt that the harbour question had not been settled. He said he would not let contracts to complete the road until it had been decided which harbour to use.

When the westerners returned to battle on the issue in March, Cochrane was under fire from his predecessor, Graham, then fresh from his by-election victory. Graham urged that Cochrane choose and quickly develop a port— which, as Cochrane had said, and Graham repeated, would allow supplies for the new road to be brought in by sea more cheaply than by the overland route.

> Cochrane: Should not the hon. gentleman have done a little something when he was in office?
> Graham: I did.
> Cochrane: There is nothing in the department to show it.

Graham: I did not make it public any more than the
hon. gentleman is doing.

By then Cochrane had parties of surveyors at both ports. He
said he hoped to make a decision on a port within two months.
Late in May he told the House the decision had been made
for Port Nelson. The route was shorter and the harbour,
although not as good, could be developed by dredging. Information made public years later indicates that at the time the
decision was still not quite final, awaiting Cochrane's own
visit that summer to the sites, with his engineers.

Western newspapers had discovered Cochrane in the previous winter. Apparently they had found in him something
after their own hearts—that is, although he was an easterner
he was also a northerner, and therefore a man whose imagin-
ation never boggled when it came to Hudson Bay. His initial
delay for re-examination had offended them a little but he
quickly made up for it by producing a pipe-dream that even
the wildest western fancy hadn't thought of earlier. As almost
a throw-in to the Hudson Bay debate in mid January
Cochrane had mentioned the difficulties of navigating Hudson
Strait, but said if they were insuperable it still wouldn't
stop the project: "A line of boats could run across Hudson
Bay to the Nottaway River in Quebec, and down through
Quebec by the National Transcontinental to the Atlantic.
This would shorten the distance from Prince Albert or Edmonton to the Atlantic by about 600 miles [meaning, that much
shorter than the Lakehead route then being used]." Two
months later a subsidy was passed to extend the National
Transcontinental to James Bay to carry this out. Quebec
followed with a provincial subsidy for that part of the line.
Even Cochrane's sturdiest antagonists in the House could only
gulp over this new proposal, called by Cochrane "a second
string to our bow". The *Toronto Star* said:

Progressive Canadians will delight in this particular
optimism by Frank Cochrane. This is the sort we like to

hear. The race is on. The present is no time to stumble over our heels.

Western papers echoed this enthusiasm.

It was a long touring summer. Borden sailed for England, where he fell under the spell of Winston Churchill, First Lord of the Admiralty, and worked out what would suit them both as a naval policy.

Early in July, Cochrane started out on a coast-to-coast, plus Arctic, trip. He stopped in North Bay to receive a presentation of a cabinet containing a 200-piece set of sterling silver from his old northern field staff from Ontario's Lands, Forests and Mines department: mining recorders, chief rangers, timber agents. From there he travelled west by private car, with a few officials and his son Wilbur. George Yates was along to handle ministerial work and carry the camera that recorded meetings with railroad officials along the way through the Kootenays and the Skeena River to Prince Rupert, down the coast by the Canadian Northern's boat, S. S. *Prince Rupert,* to Victoria, and then back east to Lake Louise, Banff, Calgary, Prince Albert, and The Pas to Winnipeg.

While on the train Cochrane received a telegram from Borden naming a date late in September when he wanted all members of cabinet to frame the government's naval policy. In Calgary and elsewhere Cochrane gave newspaper interviews on railroad affairs. In Winnipeg he and Interior Minister Bob Rogers were importuned by delegations insisting that the government make the Grand Trunk Pacific open their shops at nearby Transcona. Cochrane told a *Winnipeg Tribune* reporter buoyantly that a wireless system would be set up in Hudson Straits to help steamers keep free of pack ice. The *Manitoba Free Press* took some shots at him editorially on August 6, demanding an explanation of rumours about a technical question of the day: the grades being built into the National Transcontinental. The *Tribune* countered the next day with a lyrical forecast about how Cochrane's visit to

Hudson Bay would help produce "a site [where] now bleak sea basin waste shall flower into a populous metropolis."

A few days later, on August 10, 1912, Cochrane, Yates, and Chief Engineer Bowden were on the dock at Selkirk to board the Lake Winnipeg steamer *Lady of the Lake* for the first leg of the trip north.

They steamed north past Hecla Island, passing fishing boats manned by Icelandic farmer-fishermen who had settled much of the meadow land along the west shore of the lake. A crowd was out to meet them at Warren's Landing on the north end of Lake Winnipeg, where they changed to a smaller river steamer, the *Highlander*. In a few hours they were at Norway House and Cochrane was sitting for a Yates photo showing him in a big wicker chair on the veranda of the Hudson Bay factor's home, with the factor's family around him.

Cochrane loved this trip, Yates wrote. It reminded him of his younger days on the rivers and lakes of Northern Ontario.

The Nelson River at Norway House has a shoreline of low, curved solid rock, topped by the stunted trees common to the region. Canoes were waiting, and nine guides and paddlers had been assigned—among them Charles Wesley (who wore a derby hat), and Tonal, James, and Joseph McKay. After a sight-seeing day, the party cast off on a murky morning in cold rain.

Their route led first to the northeast. For fifteen miles a motor boat towed the line of twenty-foot canoes. Then the boat turned back and they were on their own. The flies were bad on shore, and sometimes mosquito nettings looking like beekeepers' hats were worn. On the water the hazards were the normal ones of the time and the wild territory: minor rapids to be shot, waterfalls to be portaged around. The Indians called Cochrane White Chief, and when he first picked up a paddle they thought it was more for show than anything. But, wrote George Yates later, "He personally paddled every mile of the way."

Each day in the late afternoon the canoes would go ashore

and tents would be raised and fires lighted. In pictures, Cochrane is sometimes working with the guides in loading and unloading, and sometimes sitting off to one side watching, coat off, his suspenders showing beneath his vest. His artificial leg was apparently no serious hindrance in embarking and disembarking on the rough shorelines.

Near the end of the nine-day journey sometimes sails and oars were used. One photo shows the White Chief's canoe with a sail hoisted, a tarpaulin rigged to keep off the rain, one Indian rowing, and Cochrane digging in with his paddle. He was nearly sixty at the time.

Near the end he pushed the party a little. The previous Governor General, Earl Grey, had made the same trip in ten days. Cochrane wanted to beat that record. He did. The party landed at York Factory near the mouth of the Nelson, and hard by Port Nelson, nine days after leaving Norway House. The Hudson Bay factor and his comely family were waiting, and offshore sat the government steamer *Stanley* to take the minister aboard.

Cochrane's inspection of Port Nelson along with his surveyors took a day or two. Then the journey continued north to Churchill for more conferences with engineers and survey parties. From there the party embarked on the *Stanley* for the return voyage. A heavy storm forced the ship to put in to shore once to ride it out. A few days later they entered the pack ice of Hudson Straits and took two full days to get through. After that they passed down the coast of Labrador, with icebergs always in view.

A few days before his arrival in Montreal on September 5, this news report was published:

> Hon. Frank Cochrane is nearing civilization on his way home by sea from Port Nelson. The steamer Stanley is expected daily in the Strait of Belle Isle and will proceed thence to Sydney, Cape Breton. There the Minister will be met by officials of the Intercolonial Railway and will come again in active touch with the

affairs of his department. Mr. Cochrane, it will be recalled, went over the lines of the railways in the west and the route of the Hudson Bay Railway, with the object of making himself personally familiar with the conditions, progress of construction works, etc. Reaching Hudson Bay he was met by the Stanley and proceeded to obtain from actual experience an idea of what may be expected from the water route from Port Nelson or Fort Churchill. This is the first time that a Minister of Railways in Canada has ever acted as a pathfinder for a new transportation route.

Within three weeks after he returned to Ottawa he was ready to approve the full route: 422 miles from The Pas to a point in the Nelson Estuary twenty-two miles from the river's mouth. J. D. McArthur and Company of Winnipeg, who had the original contract, soon were awarded the rest of it. In the next year 102 miles of track were laid and the schedule called for completion by midsummer in 1916. But when war came in 1914 the plan had to be changed; certain materials quickly became scarce, and the best and toughest men began to head for the armed forces. In February 1915 Cochrane told the House that the Hudson Bay route now could not be opened before 1917. But when 1917 came, the road was still only at Kettle Rapids (Mile 333). Work ground to a halt.

It was revived as a sturdy political issue in the 1920s. Mackenzie King, in trouble and needing western votes, pledged in 1926 that the Hudson Bay Railway (once again, with feeling) "would be completed without delay". This time Churchill was chosen as the terminus. On March 29, 1929, the skeleton tracks finally reached Churchill—nearly ten years after Cochrane's death.

No doubt, without the war, the road would have been completed by 1916 to Port Nelson. If so, it might have loomed as Cochrane's achievement—or as his failure. The judgment of history is that from the outset there were too many insurmountable problems to justify building the road. It has been in use now for forty years but never has lived up to the western dream. One of Cochrane's last official acts before his death was to appear as a witness in 1919 before a Senate Committee investigating (as many times before) the navigability of Hudson Bay and Strait. This committee still showed enough of the old optimism to say that the road, in the end, would be profitable. But it found that Nelson had been the wrong choice as the port.

"The selection was finally decided by me largely on the report of the engineers," Cochrane told the committee. "The tender to go to Churchill was four million dollars more than to go to Nelson and while the harbour at Churchill would be easier to develop as a small harbour, the saving would not be as much as the difference in cost of building the railroad. But before I was at Nelson, a boat drawing 20 feet had been up the river to where the harbour later was developed—and this without any work being done on the channels. I think if you look up Hansard you will find that Mr. Graham, my predecessor, said his engineer had been in favor of Nelson, the same as mine."

He had one flash of his old optimism on the subject: "The Straits are an even harder thing to overcome than the port. But I feel that with proper aids to navigation the straits can be used longer than most people at present think—both longer, and more effectively."

He delivered one other reflection on the Hudson Bay Railway in the Commons in January 1912 that has relevance today. This came after he had defended his delay, and said work would now be pushed. "I believe it is the duty of this government or any other government to open up that large section of Canada *and see what is there*," he said. "Great results have accrued from opening up country which was formerly looked upon as part of the frozen north. Such has been the case in Ontario and in the Yukon, and if for no other reason than that, I believe that it would be well worth our while to build the road to Hudson Bay. . . ."

Along or near the railroad now, served by it through branch lines and highways, are the mines at Snow Lake and one of the world's major nickel discoveries at Thompson. As an observer said when the Thompson mine was new: "A few such strikes and the Hudson Bay Railway yet may come into its own." And thus prove the value, even retroactively, of Cochrane's contention a half-century earlier that it was important to open up the country "and see what is there".

CHAPTER THIRTEEN

If this measure [Borden's plan to give $35 million outright to Britain to build three battleships] becomes law, at the end of the war we may be able to erect a monument with the simple inscription, "To the glorious memory of thirty five million dollars, lost at sea."

Stephen Leacock, early 1913

When Cochrane returned to Ottawa in September 1912 he had already been told, along with other ministers, that the first item of cabinet business would be the most controversial: the framing of Borden's Naval Aid Bill. All hands knew that this would cause a showdown in the uneasy alliance between Borden and his Quebec ministers, especially Monk. For years, including the election campaign a year earlier, Monk had denounced any form of naval aid to Britain. Cochrane's canoe trip and the voyage through the icy seas of Hudson Bay and off Labrador had left him looking tanned and well, and the long rest from routine had refreshed him. It was a good thing. The months to come were to cause unbearable strain, come close to wrecking Borden's health, and eventually send Cochrane to hospital under an assumed name (a successful device to keep this news from the press until he had recovered).

The first cabinet meeting on the matter came a few days after Cochrane's return. Borden had requested from Winston Churchill two documents to support the proposals he was about to make—simply to give Britain $35,000,000 to build three capital ships. One document was a secret assessment of the mounting armaments race in Europe. This made the flat statement that Britain no longer ruled the waves; indeed, couldn't be effectively responsible for much beyond the North Sea. To give Borden this realistic statement in writing was to enable him to persuade political friend and foe alike that Britain urgently needed help. Borden was empowered to show it privately where he deemed necessary, including to Laurier and other Liberal Privy Councillors. The second document was weaker in content, being designed for publication. Borden was dissatisfied with the second document because it didn't mention specifically that capital ships were needed, fast. (Apparently Britain wished to keep this from potential adversaries, if they hadn't already guessed the situation.)

That day both documents were read by cabinet. In the ensuing hour of discussion, the gloomy and cadaverous Monk agonized over his position in Quebec. He insisted that a plebiscite should be held, allowing the public to say yea or nay. His Quebec colleague, Nantel, agreed. Cochrane spoke against the plebiscite idea. So did other Ontario ministers and a scattered majority of other ministers. That settled it; there would be no plebiscite. Borden went ahead with the draft of his bill.

In two weeks he presented it to cabinet, where unanimous approval was recorded—although, Borden noted, Monk did not say a word. A few days later Monk resigned from the cabinet. The pressure on him had been intense from powerful English-speaking Tories in Montreal to support the naval aid bill, but more intense from rank-and-file Quebeckers to repudiate it. Quebec's opposition was being freshly whipped up by a series of speeches Laurier was making. He and other French Canadians would stand by Britain in time of danger, he was saying, but not because of any "pretended emergency".

This scoffing by Laurier at the possibility of any real danger of war persisted almost until the firing began nearly two years later.

Meanwhile, Borden was busy every day trying to prepare public ground for the naval bill before opening Parliament on November 21. Cochrane, White, and other Ontario ministers were doing what they could to whip up rank-and-file support —Cochrane during an inspection tour of the Welland Canal (about to be enlarged), and also when he spoke in Halifax to announce plans for massive harbour improvements there: a mile and a half of new harbour works including six 1,250-foot piers, immigration buildings, a grain elevator, and a railroad station. (This was Borden's territory, of course, but Cochrane shared the acclaim.)

Early in November Borden called in what he described as "several prominent members of the press" and outlined to them the contents of the secret memorandum from the Admiralty. On November 7 he showed the document to Premier McBride of British Columbia, explained his policy fully, and got McBride's support. On November 16 he gave Laurier a copy of the secret memorandum. On November 18 John Willison, editor of the *Toronto News* and a friend of Cochrane, was brought in to hear the secret details. On the day before Parliament opened, Borden gave his cabinet a preview of the speech he would make in proposing the bill a week or so later. He accepted a few suggestions for changes.

A surprise to no one in Canada, the Throne Speech's most important proposal was the Naval Aid Bill. Then Borden heard that some Quebec members were prepared to bolt the party on the question, so he met with them and got most to promise support, although others felt bound to vote against the bill.

After all this preparation, and with visitors from many parts of Canada jamming the public galleries to hear the proposals, a silly accident brought a moment of slapstick to Borden's opening speech on the bill. In his eagerness, he rose to speak before the motion introducing the bill had been read. He shoved his chair into the aisle to give himself swinging room. But at that instant the Speaker, a stickler for due process, interrupted him to put the motion. Borden sat down—forgetting he had pushed his chair away. He fell backwards and broke his glasses. Cochrane and other nearby ministers rushed to help him up. Luckily, Borden had brought another pair of glasses, because his carefully worked-out notes were quite extensive. That comic instant lives on in the history of what became one of the fiercest Commons debates of all time.

His speech was interrupted dozens of times by applause, and at the end those on his side of the House and some on the other side, as well as the packed galleries, rose and sang "Rule Britannia" and "God Save the King". (The same anthem-singing was accorded Laurier a few days later after his reply to Borden's speech at the first-reading stage.)

The long, man-destroying fight was on. It continued that month until the Christmas recess. At New Year's the Governor General showed Borden a letter from King George V, lauding the naval policy and Borden's speech. The debate resumed again on January 14. Other matters were routinely before the House from time to time but the naval bill was the big one. Amendments were voted upon and defeated. On February 27, second reading was passed and the bill went into committee for clause-by-clause consideration. Debate resumed on March 3. On that day when Laurier asked for adjournment at midnight, Borden refused. He kept refusing. That night he left others in charge a few minutes before four a.m., and returned from his bed six hours later to resume the debate. For the next two weeks, except for two days, March 8 and 9, the debate on the Naval Aid Bill went on continuously night and day. Borden, Cochrane, White, Perley, Hughes, and other ministers worked in shifts. So did the members, on both sides. On Friday, March 14, and the next day, the debate at times came close to physical combat. There were wild scenes of disorder with tempers frayed by long hours and, sometimes, strong drink. As the spring dragged on into April, Borden began to consider using closure, if he had to: a parliamentary device to end debate arbitrarily, by force of numbers.

First he tried to get Laurier to fix a date for third reading of the bill, promising the Liberals they could have all the time for debate that Laurier desired. Laurier declined to make a deal. By now fatigue and strain were taking a serious physical toll on both sides, although mostly on the government because it had to be sure to keep a majority in the House at all times in case the Liberals forced a snap vote. Borden was suffering from extremely troublesome carbuncles (which are like boils but bigger and more painful). He had them lanced when he could. Twice he was called from bed to hurry to the House in emergencies, appearing there with his head and neck swathed in bandages. His ministers, especially the older ones, were exhausted. Cochrane was ill enough early in April that one Tory member, W. H. Bennett from Midland, suggested in a letter to Borden that he would be available if Cochrane's health forced him to leave the cabinet.

On April 9, Borden decided finally to push the bill through by whatever means possible. His doctor tended him before he went to the Commons. He told his caucus at noon what was to come: the first stage of enforcing closure. It was done. Even so, under the complicated rules of debate, and while the eventual fate of the bill in the Commons was now sealed, it was possible for the Opposition to prolong the debate for another month. The bill finally was passed through Committee at 3.30 a.m. on a Saturday morning, May 10, and passed its third Commons reading five days later without the use of the closure motion that Borden had as a hole card.

But remember the Senate? The bill still had to pass there— and did not. In Bruce Hutchison's book *Mr. Prime Minister* he wrote succinctly: "In a Senate dominated by Laurier's appointees . . . the naval bill was rejected on Laurier's instructions." Laurier denied this charge of personal intervention at the time, and again in 1914 in the Commons. But Borden related in his memoirs that even before the bill was out of the

Commons, Sir George Ross, the Liberal leader in the Senate, had been in touch with the cabinet about proposed amendments that would make the bill acceptable to the Senate. Ross said he had the support of leading Liberals in the Senate. Borden returned word that if Sir George could guarantee Laurier's acquiescence, the government would be willing to discuss amendments. Laurier refused. Borden: "In the end, Sir Wilfrid insisted upon the rejection of the bill, giving to his friends in the Senate the choice between that course and his resignation."

The toll that six months of fierce, and finally fruitless, parliamentary fighting had taken on all the adversaries can be imagined. Cochrane and his wife retained their home in Toronto but had an apartment a few minutes away from his office. He wasn't much of a drinker, with his Methodist background, so he didn't have that "out" as a way of relaxing—as many of his colleagues did. Even his favourite indoor relaxation, playing cards with his wife and friends, found no place in his life that year.

He beat a path from the Commons to his office to his apartment, taking part not only in the naval debate but in dozens of others affecting his own department—bills, subsidies, housekeeping amendments. He also followed closely the progress of the royal commission that he and Borden had set up to investigate charges of profiteering in the construction of the National Transcontinental during Laurier's time, launched plans for the new Welland ship canal and for the modernization of Halifax harbour, fought off requests for patronage, defended himself in the House constantly against reports of patronage on government railways (even though most of the Opposition members seemed to trust his often-expressed opposition to patronage, and to accept what he told them).

In addition, most of the nation's railroads were in trouble, including the government-owned Intercolonial in the Maritimes. But by then Cochrane was taking it in hand. He appointed a new general manager, F. P. Gutelius (an American-born British subject who had worked in various capacities for the C.P.R. and also was a sharply inquiring commissioner in the National Transcontinental inquiry.) They raised rates, consolidated staff, and improved the Intercolonial's financial position. This success first indicated to some of Cochrane's powerful cabinet colleagues that one solution to other railroad difficulties might be some form of public ownership or control.

In the middle stages of the Naval Aid Bill debate, Sir William Mackenzie of the Canadian Northern came to Ottawa, desperate for funds. G. R. Stevens wrote in his book, *Canadian National Railways*: "He was astonished by his reception. No hostile inquisitors, no prying auditors, awaited him; instead, the Minister of Railways greeted him not with guarantees but with cash in hand. He was offered a subsidy of $12,000 a mile on 1,170 miles of line [Ottawa–Port Arthur and Edmonton–Yellowhead] and $6,400 a mile on 250 miles between Toronto and Ottawa. In return he was asked to assign to the Government common stock of the Canadian Northern to the nominal value of $7,000,000. . . ."

Mackenzie accepted. Cochrane piloted the measure through Commons although the Liberals forced seven recorded votes, losing them all. The Senate also approved. "No one could mistake the significance," Stevens wrote. With the government a shareholder, snug groups of railroad capitalists no longer would have a free hand in this major transcontinental line. It was the thin edge of the wedge that eventually brought Canadian National Railways into being a few years later, an historical move in which Cochrane had a leading part.

He travelled for three weeks through Northern Ontario with Hearst that summer, consolidating his protégé's hold on what had been Cochrane's political fiefdom. But everywhere else he turned that year, strain piled on strain. All of it was loaded on top of those long and sleepless months of the naval bill debate. Early in November he suffered what was believed at first to have been a nervous breakdown. It was kept so secret that it is uncertain where he was when it happened, the circumstances, the exact day, or any other detail. In reference material it shows first in a letter Borden wrote from Virginia, where he had gone because "I was on the verge of exhaustion." Apparently news followed him quickly that he was not the only one.

His letter was dated "The Greenbrier", White Sulphur Springs, West Virginia, November 7, 1913. The words and phrases shown in parentheses had been crossed out but were readable.

> My Dear Mrs. Cochrane:
> We are greatly distressed to learn that your husband is so seriously ill. It is most unfortunate that he did not give up (his) work immediately after the session and place himself then in the hands of a capable physician. His too insistent devotion to duty prevented him from taking that course and his wonderful pluck and courage prevented me from realizing how ill he must have been. (Not only did he bring great) Apart from the great personal strength which he brings to the government (but) his (personal) splendid qualities of mind and heart have endeared him to all his colleagues and especially to myself. We hope and pray that entire abstention from work and worry of any kind may result in marked and continued improvement and that his health and strength may be once more fully restored.
> Kindest remembrance and every good wish, believe me, Dear Mrs. Cochrane,
>
> > Yours faithfully,
> > R. L. Borden.

Alice Cochrane's reply was from Toronto, November 13, 1913.

> My Dear Mr. Borden:
> Your letter with kind enquiries about Mr. Cochrane came a few days ago and would have been answered sooner but I was obliged to go to Ottawa for a day. After considerable pressure we got Mr. Cochrane to consult with a specialist and after a thorough examination and consultation he gave in to treatment, and going up for a time for a perfect rest. He is now in

Wellesley Hospital, Toronto, in bed all the time. His place of abode is a state secret and [he is] known as Mr. Starr. I am at my mother's but spend all day with him. Both doctors very much pleased with the progress he is making and now they have every hope of his being as strong as ever again. They told me he must stay here for two weeks but have not decided or told me what he must do later more than he must be very careful and to rest and diet. He is very contented having given in more gracefully than I had first hoped for. Dr. Reid is going to see him Saturday. He is allowed a few visitors but so far we have succeeded in keeping his illness from the newspapers and we trust we can until he is about again. Thanking you for your kind letter and with best wishes for your own return to health in which Mr. Cochrane joins.

> Sincerely,
> Alice Cochrane.

This exchange was rather less pointed than some others on the subject. The illness was accentuated by exhaustion, but more importantly, it was the first indication that Cochrane was suffering from the early stages of Bright's disease, a kidney malady. Agriculture Minister Martin Burrell wrote to Borden: "Mrs. Cochrane told my wife confidentially that though it was a close call for Bright's Disease, he had come under [the doctor's] hands just in time." Finance Minister White wrote: "I am deeply concerned about Cochrane but am hoping that his kidney trouble may turn out to be acute and not chronic. If the latter I am afraid he is in for a hard time." In another letter, November 18, White was a little more hopeful, but "I agree with you that it would be most desirable that he should have several months rest. Dr. Reid has taken hold of the department with his usual energy." Borden's reply, a few days later: "The latest reports respecting our colleague are more encouraging and I think there is every reason to hope that with some months rest his health may be so restored as to enable him to continue in public life for some years. It was most unfortunate that he did not consult a competent physician six or twelve months ago. His tendency to magnify details of the administration and the consequent worry and strain have made his task, which is severe for any man, a very tremendous one for him."

This illness was with Cochrane for the remaining six years of his life, was responsible for denying him the post he felt would crown his career in public life, and was a factor in his death.

CHAPTER FOURTEEN

When Cochrane left hospital late in 1913, his illness reported publicly only in retrospect, he visited in Sudbury for a few days just after Christmas. Early in February 1914 he announced that as soon as he could get his estimates through the House, he would leave for the Mediterranean for a rest recommended by his doctors. He left in March, with Dr. J. D. Reid taking over Railways and Canals on an acting basis.

A day or two after Cochrane landed in Liverpool, in writing to thank Borden for sending "such a kind message to the boat", he showed that he didn't leave politics far behind, ever. He was urging Borden to approach a Montrealer named Ballantyne, a Liberal who had left his party over Reciprocity, and try to get him as a Conservative candidate. "It strikes me he would have a great effect on a good many Liberals who supported us the last time. If you could get in touch with him as soon as possible, and engage him, it would be a good thing."

It seems likely that about this time Cochrane was once again under pressure from his wife to leave politics altogether. Whitney had been ill most of the winter, and left hospital about the time the Cochranes reached the south of France. (Sir George Ross died in Ottawa that same month.) Cochrane's correspondence from the party organization in Ontario obliquely mentioned from time to time that Whitney's illness was so serious that a new leader might have to be found. There were rumours that if Whitney had to step down, Cochrane would be his choice.

When Cochrane returned to Canada late in May, Whitney was still weak but insisted on working as usual, against doctor's orders. Cochrane himself seemed full of his old vigour, and assured an interviewer that this was so. He visited Whitney in Toronto and returned to Ottawa on May 17, and, one newspaper of May 18 said, "this morning plunged at once into the arrears of work at his office. He was at his desk by eight o'clock and was overwhelmed by callers all morning. . . . Mr. Cochrane says he feels as well as he ever did and is completely recovered. He will take his seat in the House today."

That was the summer the First World War began. Only a few months earlier Cochrane had heard the final death-rattle of the Naval Aid Bill. It was dead and gone, but was still being debated any time a chance arose to lambaste the Liberals in the Senate for killing it. Such a chance occurred when Borden read into the record a dispatch from the German newspaper *Hamburger Nachrichten*, noting that "the decision of the Canadian Senate [in killing the bill] means at any rate a heavy moral and material loss for the defence of the Empire, for Mr. Borden's promise had been foolishly enough counted on."

Laurier then defended the Senate's actions in words he probably wished later he had not spoken:

> The Bill which was brought in last session was not even a measure of emergency, although it was so called. . . . Emergency? Who speaks today of emergency? . . . Twelve months and more have passed since he [Borden] saw the German peril. He saw Germany almost ready to jump at the throat of Great Britain. He saw clouds on

the horizon; he saw these clouds rent by lightning; he heard the murmurs and the rumbling of the distant thunder. But my right hon. friend today may live in peace. The atmosphere is pure, the sky is clear. . . . We know now how much the country and the Empire and the civilized world has been deceived upon the question of so-called emergency.

Bruce Hutchison later called this speech "a fit of blindness and pique".

The session ended and Borden was at a Muskoka resort late in July 1914 when he was summoned by a telegram from his secretary warning him that war was near. He boarded a fast motor boat, caught a train to Ottawa, summoned his cabinet, cabled to London Canada's offer to help Britain, passed an incredible series of orders-in-council to make such help possible, and called Parliament to sit August 18.

On the night of August 3, Sir Wilfrid Laurier arrived in the capital, still hoping there would be no war. But if one came, "the policy of the Liberal party under such painful circumstances is well known. I have often declared that if the Mother Country were ever in danger or if danger even threatened, Canada would render assistance to the full extent of her power. In view of the critical nature of the full situation I have cancelled all my meetings. Pending such great questions there should be a truce of party strife."

At 8.55 p.m. on August 4, a cable arrived at the council chamber where Borden, Cochrane, White, Hughes, Perley, and most of the other cabinet members were meeting. The cable said Britain was at war. Under the conditions of belonging to the British Empire at the time, that meant Canada was also at war.

While Sam Hughes bustled off in all directions to perform the remarkable feat of mobilizing (at Valcartier, Quebec), training (a little), and embarking 30,000 men for Britain within two months after the declaration of war, one major burden of the rest of the Canadian war effort obviously was about to fall on the Canadian railways. Cochrane was back at work night and day again.

Toronto visitors then brought him other upsetting news. The stresses of Whitney's illness and his refusal to convalesce were endangering him once more. He was under doctor's care, but wouldn't stay away from his office. He suffered another attack and Cochrane was told that the end was near. On September 25, Whitney died of a cerebral hemorrhage—and Cochrane, quite suddenly, as well as being busy from early morning until late at night mobilizing the railways for their role in the war effort, had been handed again his baton as one of the callers of the political tune in Ontario.

A telephone call was made from Toronto to Cochrane in the early afternoon of September 25 to report Whitney's death. Another call, later in the day, was from Cochrane's old Ontario colleague, Dr. R. A. Pyne, education minister and the second most senior member of the Ontario cabinet. The senior man was J. J. Foy, the Attorney General, but he was seriously ill at the time.

A few hours after Whitney's death, his private secretary had approached Dr. Pyne with a sealed envelope inscribed "To be opened immediately after my death. J. P. W."

In it were two notes in Whitney's own handwriting. Pyne revealed the contents to Cochrane. One, undated, stated rather mysteriously that upon Whitney's death, "Dr. Pyne should take such steps as will put the fact of my death beyond all possibility of doubt." (Whitney apparently had a fear of lapsing into a deep coma, as had happened during his illness, and being buried alive.)

The other bore the address of Whitney's residence at 113 St. George Street, and was dated May 17, the day on which Cochrane visited Whitney in Toronto. While there is no evidence of what was said during the discussion between the two men when they met that day, it would be not unreasonable to assume that one of the subjects was covered in the note Whitney wrote. Cochrane might even have seen it at the time:

The document was headed simply "Memo" and read:

> In the event of my death I desire to say to my colleagues that, in my opinion, Mr. Foy should succeed me as Prime Minister.
>
> In the event of his declining, an effort should be made to get Mr. Cochrane to accept the position.
>
> If this cannot be brought about then, in my opinion, Mr. Hearst or Mr. Lucas should be chosen. This is all merely my opinion which I give for what it is worth, but the reasons behind my opinion will at once occur to those who give consideration to the matter. Among them are the geographical position of Mr. Hearst which gives him a great advantage over others. Mr. Foy deserves anything that our party can give him, and there is no stronger man than Mr. Cochrane in the province.

There was no public speculation at the time as to the reasoning Sir James was sure would "at once occur to those who give consideration to the matter" because the document was revealed only to the cabinet. It was placed in the Ontario Archives only in 1952 after being found in Sir William Hearst's papers.

But there was naturally newspaper speculation on the succession. Political commentators of the time felt there were five major candidates: Cochrane, Adam Beck of Ontario Hydro, Provincial Secretary W. J. Hanna, Hearst, and Provincial Treasurer I. B. Lucas. They believed if a convention were held, Lucas would win. But as often happens, the pundits were not in possession of enough inside facts to be very close in their guesses.

The more-informed line of reasoning among the cabinet ministers, who saw the note and kept its secret, went this way. Whitney knew that Foy was in poor health and would not accept, but felt he owed him first mention. He also probably knew that Cochrane felt committed to Ottawa. Lucas had talked of returning to private life. So of the four names mentioned he was really picking Cochrane's longtime protégé, Hearst, who since taking over Cochrane's post in Lands,

Forests, and Mines in 1911 had enjoyed Cochrane's constant support and had become Whitney's confidant.

Brian D. Tennyson's 1964 paper on Hearst's succession, published in *Ontario History*, suggested that Cochrane's "invisible hand" could be seen in events surrounding Whitney's death. Certain facts of political life had to be dealt with, as usual. One was that Adam Beck, the minister without portfolio whose policy of publicly owned utilities had given him high popularity throughout the province, had to be won over at least to acceding to Hearst's elevation. Wrote Tennyson: "Cochrane's invisible hand could be discerned immediately when it was announced from Ottawa [the day before Whitney died, but when death was expected at any moment] that J. S. Hendrie would succeed J. M. Gibson as Lieutenant-governor. Hendrie, a minister without portfolio and member of the Ontario Hydro Commission, had frequently opposed Beck's plans on the commission. Therefore, Beck and his wing of the party were to be placated with the appointment to the commission of someone who would be more co-operative."

It is also possible that other influence was brought to bear by Cochrane on Beck and the others not to oppose Whitney's (and Cochrane's) choice. Lucas, apparently having reconsidered his return to private life, later was appointed attorney general and named to the Hydro Commission to replace Hendrie. Beck was the only member of the cabinet who resigned on Hearst's accession to the premiership. He said that in running the Hydro he wished to be wholly independent of political parties. But it was commonly believed that he simply refused to serve under the younger and less experienced Hearst.

Others, recalling the impact Cochrane had made on Ontario Conservative politics, his handling of judicial, senatorial and other appointments, and his long championship of Hearst as another strong man from the North, simply re-read Whitney's words, "there is no stronger man in the province than Mr. Cochrane," and let it go at that.

CHAPTER FIFTEEN

> Mr. Cochrane, whose strong antagonism to the Grand
> Trunk Railway was quite manifest, precipitated some
> heated discussions and rather violent scenes in connec-
> tion with the affairs of that railway and of the Grand
> Trunk Pacific Railway. White and I were agreed and
> determined that nothing should be done to injure the
> credit of the two railways.
>
> *Robert Laird Borden, His Memoirs*

If White and Borden were put by Cochrane into the position
of defending the Grand Trunk, his attitude must have been
violent indeed. Borden himself always had ranged somewhere
between cool and frosty toward the Grand Trunk. Some of this
dated from the 1908 federal election campaign. Borden
thought the Grand Trunk openly had favoured the Liberals,
leading him to write privately that if the Grand Trunk wanted
a fight, the Conservative party would be glad to oblige. There
had been some company partisanship in the 1911 election as
well that stuck in his mind.

White's sentiments against the Grand Trunk also were
known, partly owing to his connection with the same Toronto
financial circles as those frequented by Sir William Mackenzie
and Sir Donald Mann, owners of the Canadian Northern.

But Cochrane? "Heated discussions and rather violent scenes" did not seem in his line, except as an indication of one thing: what he felt to be bad faith, or bad business.

This inference can be drawn from a passage in G. R. Stevens' book on the history of the C.N.R., when he summarized Borden's cabinet as not outstanding, except that "in this miscellany there were two tough and able men—Francis Cochrane, Minister of Railways and Canals, and Thomas White, Minister of Finance." Stevens also mentioned Arthur Meighen and R. B. Bennett, and said, "These four were destined to become the inner circle on railway matters. Cochrane was set on seeing that the government got value for every dollar expended. White wanted more than that; he wanted some return on government aid extended to railways in the past."

These ministerial imperatives by Cochrane and White added up to a tall order; at the time two billion dollars was invested in Canadian railways, and half of that had come from the public purse.

Cochrane's balance-the-books techniques proved particularly maddening to Maritimers, mainly because the Intercolonial was the one road subject to direct government control. He unflaggingly supported the tough general-managership of the Intercolonial by his hand-picked man, F. P. Gutelius, against the anguished cries of Maritimes members, Tories as well as Grits. Gutelius cleaned house by firing people where he found incompetence—no matter what political party the man belonged to. This was almost unheard-of in all Intercolonial history. Meanwhile Cochrane had a committee investigating charges of political partisanship (this phrase really meant Liberal political partisanship of an open nature). If the charges were considered valid the man was removed. But over the years when Liberals protested in the Commons, Cochrane once replied,

I have not dismissed one-tenth as many during my

whole term of office as the honourable gentlemen opposite dismissed [when they controlled the Intercolonial].
As to patronage, I am satisfied that I cannot be accused
of running the railway in that interest. The criticism of
the people on my own side of the House is that I give no
weight to such considerations. I feel that as Minister of
Railways I am not representing the Conservative party
alone but have in charge the interests of the whole
people and I have acted accordingly.

In the Commons he got the same hot complaints over his
interpretation of a Borden campaign promise to buy up branch
lines in the Maritimes. He would only buy good-paying propo-
sitions, he said, thus outraging owners of lines that were limping along with poor roadbeds and battered rolling stock, looking forward to selling at a profit to the government. As G. R.
Stevens put it: "Some of the Maritimes Tories, after their long
sojourn in the wilderness, expected that the fleshpots of patronage would be swung over the fires once more. . . . It was to no
avail."

Sometimes Cochrane's methods were such that Maritimers
asked Borden to intervene. In 1913 New Brunswick's Conservative government passed a resolution and sent it to Cochrane protesting his plans to close a twenty-mile branch line
between Chatham Junction and Blackville. Cochrane's terse
letter in reply said: "If the legislature is prepared to make
good the deficit in running trains over the branch . . . I shall
be very glad indeed to see that the service is continued."

New Brunswick Tories took this up immediately with their
man in Ottawa, J. D. Hazen, who had left the New Brunswick premiership to become Borden's Minister of Marine,
Fisheries, and Naval Services. Hazen was told by one prominent New Brunswick Tory, "I want to say to you that as far as
I hear, I think Mr. Cochrane is injuring the party in every
county through which the Intercolonial runs, and I am very
fearful that we cannot afford to be losing ground where we
ought to be making ground very rapidly." (Meaning, making
political ground by use of patronage and buying up unprofit-

able branch lines, rather than closing them.) Hazen went to Borden with the complaints.

Borden did discuss the matter with Cochrane. No record of their conversation exists, but presumably Borden's reaction would be much as it was in a letter to Borden's old leader and patron, Sir Charles Tupper. According to G. R. Stevens, Tupper "regarded patronage as a legitimate instrument of party discipline, and he believed in material rewards for his supporters." When he tried to have Borden intervene with Cochrane to fire Gutelius and restore to power in the Inter-colonial his own old hands David Pottinger as manager and P. S. Archibald as chief engineer, Borden replied politely, ". . . If I hold Mr. Cochrane responsible for the successful management of the road it will be necessary, of course, to give him a pretty free hand. . . ."

But these matters were relatively small game. The Grand Trunk and the Canadian Northern were the major problems. The Canadian Northern had been owned entirely by Macken-zie and Mann until 1913 when Cochrane asked for and received on behalf of the government $7,000,000 in stock in return for some new financial support. (See Chapter 13.) Mackenzie and Mann were in trouble, but the railway experts in Borden's cabinet didn't seem to feel that the partners had any real fault except over-ambition. The Grand Trunk was a different case. There were no clubby Toronto connections here, no personal friendships such as the one between Mackenzie and Cochrane—which resulted in no known impropriety but did make negotiations easier. The Grand Trunk's shareholders numbered 100,000 or so. Head office was in London, England. At the Grand Trunk's shareholders meetings those who openly counselled against any truck or trade with the Canadian government had been known to receive ovations.

The major trouble the Grand Trunk faced was the result of a deal it had made with Laurier's government in 1904. Laurier's grand plan for the National Transcontinental had been that the government would build the road from Moncton to Winnipeg, and on completion the Grand Trunk would take it over and operate it—at an annual rent equalling 3 per cent of the construction costs. These costs had been estimated at $30,000 a mile, which would have made the rental reasonable. But the costs now were approaching $100,000 a mile, and the Grand Trunk (although it kept this fact private) simply could not handle a rental cost at that level.

There could have been a way out—renegotiation. It was mid 1912 when Cochrane first requested the Grand Trunk to take over the eastern division and operate it according to the 1904 agreement. That summer of 1912, the Staunton-Gutelius Royal Commission investigating construction costs on the National Transcontinental was well under way. It was already known that there had been great waste. If the Grand Trunk then had said to Cochrane, "Sure, we'll do it, but we shouldn't have to pay an exorbitant rent based on government waste," there would have been sympathetic listeners. Instead, the Grand Trunk fell back on a technicality: the eastern division was not yet complete, and their agreement was to begin operation only on completion. They declined to take over completed sections piecemeal.

In 1914, when the Staunton-Gutelius Commission did make public its unhappy account of everything from sloppy management to outright theft, the Grand Trunk might have moved again to have the agreement re-written, but did not. G. R. Stevens speculates that the company's own building record on the western division under the Grand Trunk Pacific was so bad that it decided not to try to capitalize on the government's similar troubles.

All the same, the agreement was there—and in 1915 Cochrane, having travelled the whole route from Moncton to Winnipeg himself and finding only some terminals and the Quebec bridge incomplete, accepted the word of the National Transcontinental engineers that within the terms of the agreement the railroad itself was completed. On January 13, he asked the Grand Trunk Pacific to take over the eastern division forthwith, stating that the cost "to date" on which rental would be based was $172,023,191. E. J. Chamberlin, president of the company, once again contended that it wasn't completed. Part of the original deal had been that the government's chief engineer, Gordon Grant, and the G.T.P.'s chief engineer, H. A. Woods, were to agree when completion was reached. Grant, the government man, stated his approval in a letter (either innocent or crafty) asking Woods of G.T.P. to sign the enclosed statement to that effect—". . . in duplicate, and you are at liberty to retain one of the copies for the company." Woods didn't sign. "Your opinion in this regard is different from my own," he wrote to Grant, politely.

But the real crux of the matter—and this is probably what made Cochrane, White, and Meighen so adamant later—was expressed in a private and confidential letter Chamberlin wrote to Borden. While standing on the "completion" technicality publicly, he gave the true reason to Borden privately: the G.T.P. was scraping bottom, just barely getting by on its western operation. To take over the eastern division, with its meagre earnings and high rent, would put the company another unbearable $6 million a year in the hole.

G. R. Stevens noted that "When Borden placed Chamberlin's admission before the cabinet, protracted discussions ensued." Some ministers thought the G.T.P. should get a break because the deal with Laurier had been a bad one. But: "Some were out for blood." This group obviously included Cochrane, whose department already was operating some sections of the line that the G.T.P. had refused to take over in 1912. His precise attitude in cabinet was known only to his colleagues, but one public statement he made was a strong indication.

During a goodwill tour of the North by Ontario's Premier Hearst early in 1915, Cochrane met the party at Cochrane, Ontario, in his private railroad car, *Nipissing*. He arrived just in time to run into an indignation meeting. Citizens in the main-line town were irate, telling the visiting potentates what they thought of a government that would pour nearly $200 million into a railroad and then let it rust unused.

Hearst was howled down and so was a member of his cabinet, the Hon. Howard Ferguson. The meeting was described in newspaper accounts as being on the verge of a riot when Cochrane rose and waited for the hubbub to subside. The time limit for the Grand Trunk Pacific's taking up its lease was May 1, he said, and: "If the Grand Trunk does not take action, I promise you that something will be done." That was all. He sat down.

Back in the Commons he made ready for the next move. Somebody had to run the railroad. On March 31, 1915, he introduced an amendment to the National Transcontinental Railway Act, telling the House, "The object of this resolution is to take authority to operate the Transcontinental Railway from Moncton to Winnipeg, providing the Grand Trunk Pacific Railway company do not enter into a lease to do so. . . ." He also wanted running rights from Superior Junction to the Lakehead, to hook up the N.T.R. with the grain terminals there. The road was ready for operation, he said, and "The Government have no desire to operate this road, and we are willing and anxious that the Grand Trunk Pacific shall enter into an arrangement for operating it. . . ." But if that didn't happen, he had to be ready.

This provoked a rather fantastic debate, covering fifty-eight pages in Hansard. Graham and Cochrane carried the main adversary positions in the early going. Laurier was up and down dozens of times, as was Meighen. The main Liberal thrust was that the company was right; the road was not completed. Cochrane's argument was that it was complete enough to run on, and that the Grand Trunk Pacific itself had collected government subsidies—claiming completion—on sections of the western division that were in the same state, or even less complete, than the eastern division was at present. "If they say their end is complete I say our end is complete," Cochrane said. There was agreement sometimes during the debate, but mainly there were just hours and hours of partisan verbiage adding up to the same position: that if the Grand Trunk Pacific wouldn't take over the road, the government would have to do the job itself.

There was one nice irony at the end, late one night. The tens of thousands of words trying to define completion had all died away. Cochrane's bill had just passed first reading. The House went into Committee of Supply. The first item was $5,000,000 for N.T.R. construction on the line that the government had been arguing all along was complete!

> Laurier: What is that for?
> Cochrane [he must have been at least smiling]: I am not going back on my statement [about the road's being complete]. We claim it is for construction, and there will be a lot of things to complete five years from now—yes, ten years from now.
> Laurier: Thirty years from now.
> Cochrane: Fifty years from now.

In all of Hansard's fifty-eight pages of debate that day Borden's name didn't appear. A few days earlier he had received a message that his mother, nearing her ninetieth year, was very ill. A special train was organized immediately to carry him, in twenty-five and a half hours, to his old family home in Grand Pré where she died and was buried. So Borden was standing by her graveside that afternoon of March 31, while Cochrane and Meighen were carrying the government arguments as the lengthy Grand Trunk debate ranged on.

The bill went through. When Grand Trunk Pacific let the May deadline pass, the government took over. Train service began between Superior Junction and Quebec on June 1. On July 15 the first Toronto-Winnipeg train over the line, now operated by Canadian Government Railways, steamed into Winnipeg. Cochrane's promise had been kept and was to lead a few years later to the government's taking over both the Grand Trunk Pacific and the Canadian Northern and putting them in with the Intercolonial and other government lines under the name of Canadian National Railways.

Cochrane's two sons, Wilbur and Ogden, were both army officers by 1915—and his own health had not recovered from the serious illness of 1913. Nearly four years of intensive work since 1911 had been hard on almost all of Borden's ministers, and was to be harder yet. Some resigned, but none for health reasons. Pelletier and Nantel, both from Quebec, left the cabinet in December 1914, and in 1915 Postmaster General T. Chase Casgrain threatened to resign if Cochrane did not order work started immediately on the much-disputed (as to site) Quebec terminal of the National Transcontinental. Cochrane made no such order, with site negotiations still under way, but Casgrain stayed on. The other ministers, even to the youngest, White, were becoming deathly weary. As Borden was to write later, "The strain upon my ministers since August, 1914, is not to be measured in years. It has left its effect on every member of the administration and notably upon myself."

Yet the business of politics as well as of government had to go on. Examples abound in the records of the time. V. Châteauvert of Quebec was claiming $58,000 for some minor and useless surveys on the National Transcontinental. Casgrain put the claim to Borden. Borden sent it to Cochrane. Cochrane shot it down with the comment that the man who had been supposed to be chief engineer on the survey company had only been paid $500 for three years' work—so it couldn't have been worth $58,000 to the company that employed him. Or, as Cochrane wrote to Borden, "This will give you a pretty fair idea of the standing of the people who are now pressing the claim." Châteauvert argued that the claim had been refused originally by the Laurier government because the company was made up of Conservatives. Cochrane: "Hardly. Prominent Liberals are in this company." Borden was very polite in his rejection because Casgrain was a sponsor of the supplicant and Borden didn't have support to spare in Quebec.

Late in 1915, Romeo Langlais, president of the Quebec district Conservative association, complained about lack of a voice in handing out jobs in the railways, the harbour commission, the militia department, and the battlefields commission which (unkindest cut) "gives all its cases to a Liberal advocate." Borden passed it along to Cochrane for comment on the railways part.

Cochrane replied:

> Dear Sir Robert:
> ... Mr. Langlais is either very unfair or misinformed. When the time came to organize the services on the transcontinental from Quebec west, I submitted the applications for employment to Messrs. Casgrain and Blondin [Quebeckers in the cabinet] and asked them to recommend to us all the ones [men] required, with the exception of the higher officials.
> I did not feel it in the interest of either the road or the public that executive appointments such as superintendent and engineers should be required as purely political patronage. We are obliged to appoint some men at least from the standpoint of ability, but some of our Quebec friends seem to have merely one qualification.

That qualification being, of course, politics. In such situations, Borden seethed in private, but his letters were models of my dear Mr. Châteauvert this and my dear Mr. Langlais that. Cochrane never lost a chance to speak out precisely, and sometimes quite snappishly.

Once he remarked to a friend that the population in Canada, listed then at less than 10,000,000, was really a lot bigger and he could prove it.

"How?" the friend asked.

"Since assuming office," Cochrane said, "I have had more than ten million applications from Canadians who are looking for government jobs."

He was among the hawks in cabinet that summer of 1915 who wanted Borden to dissolve Parliament and call an election. They said the Canadian war record up to then was good:

the First Contingent had distinguished itself in France, and a second contingent was trained and ready. The government could legally go until 1916 before an election, but the political situation might not be as good then. Borden resisted this urging. He was reluctant to push the country into an election at a time when the war effort was so important. He went against the majority of his cabinet and decided to wait until 1916. (In 1916, Laurier agreed to a year's extension, so the next election actually wasn't held until 1917.)

Many cabinet ministers had sons in the services, and some members had lost sons in action. Cochrane, depressed and in poor health near the end of 1915 (in which he had travelled 8,400 miles on inspection trips), was greatly fond of his robust older son, Wilbur, who knew the forests and mines as well as his father did. But the minister had a different and maybe deeper attachment to his younger son, Ogden, a frail youth whose health had never been good. In December of 1915 Cochrane said in Ottawa that his department would have no legislation to present in the coming session, no subsidies would be granted (not many railways were being built any more, or even ballyhooed), no bonds would be guaranteed. He reported good progress on the new $50,000,000 Welland ship canal. Temporary financial props, based on current expenses, had been arranged for the railroads that constituted his major headaches, and he could see the inevitable time coming when the Grand Trunk Pacific would have to be dealt with finally, and the Canadian Northern, too.

But he said nothing of that part of the future; simply that he was going to Europe to see his sons at the front. It was one of the few times that he availed himself of ministerial privilege for private reasons. He sailed from New York just before Christmas, and a month later returned to London from visiting Wilbur and Ogden on the Western Front.

He was met by Sir Max Aitken (later Lord Beaverbrook), who was armed with a private letter from R. B. Bennett about Cochrane. Bennett had asked Sir Max to see that

Cochrane met Prime Minister Bonar Law, Lloyd George, and others, and to ensure that he registered at Buckingham Palace and, if possible, saw the King. Bennett also wrote a rare appreciation of Cochrane, for Sir Max's benefit:

> Please remember that he is the really strong man in the Government and is responsible for our carrying 72 out of 86 seats in Ontario at the last election. . . . May I add that Mr. Cochrane is a man of simple tastes, does not smoke or drink, says little and thinks much. His hold upon the electorate of Ontario arises from the fact that he is direct, *honest*, a rare thing in Canada.
>
> If there are any real big steamship or transportation men you know please see he meets them.
>
> Remember that he hates the "gaudy show and tinsel of life"—He likes to know what is being done and who is doing it. A great silent man with a vision of the future of Canada which he cannot express.

Cochrane caught cold at the front. Early in February 1916 he stepped off the S.S. *Baltic* in New York, so ill that he had to go straight to Toronto for treatment and rest for two weeks before he was well enough to go to the southern United States with his wife and family to convalesce.

Back in Ottawa, he returned to work but only at half speed. Borden in his diary on May 31, 1916, penned a rundown of conditions, mental and physical, in his cabinet. White was in great consternation as to the general financial situation; "Cochrane unable to deal effectively with his department because of ill health; Burrell almost incapacitated; Reid absent and ill." (Reid had been Cochrane's back-up man in Railways and Canals since 1913.) On the next day Borden added to the record that Rogers wanted to quit and that he himself, the prime minister, was "very tired and weary of this life". But he also noted that he had disposed of much correspondence that day.

One example of that correspondence may indicate why he was so tired and weary. And part of why Cochrane was, as well. There had been some elections in Quebec.

Letter from Alphonse Bernier, of Levis, to Borden:

As you have known, very probably, I have been beaten in my County of Levis. . . .

I have brought to my county very important works, such as the new Dry Docks, the new Lauzon Engineering Company, which manufactures shells for the Allies.

I was quite sure of the majority of 500 until a quarter to five o'clock on the poll day.

What are the reasons for my defeat?

Perhaps it may be the bilingual question. [Ontario was insisting on English being used for instruction in all its schools, including many in eastern Ontario which were predominantly French.] But surely it is due to the employees, from top to bottom, of the Intercolonial Railway and Transcontinental Railway. All of them are sure . . . that they cannot be removed, for any reasons whatever. All the foremen of the Public Works in Levis, for instance, the new Dry Dock, of which M. P. Davis are contractors, the workers of the Harbour Commission in Quebec, are all Liberals, and all the workers of George T. Davie and Son, which employ another 1,000 employees have worked and voted against me.

I have to lay before you those reasons for my defeat: your Minister [of Railways and Canals] never took any care of my election during the five weeks which preceded it.

Memo, private, Cochrane to Borden, after Cochrane read that letter:

Dear Sir Robert:

. . . Since the change of Government the appointments at Levis have, I believe, been made largely on Mr. Bernier's recommendations.

If they did not vote for their benefactors I do not see how he should blame the Minister of Railways.

I take it for granted he does not expect us to attempt to coerce the men. We do not tolerate partisan interference in politics on the part of our employees, and the employees would not tolerate any interference with the right to vote as they please.

CHAPTER SIXTEEN

> Mr. Cochrane's retirement may come at any time.
> His health precludes all possibility of his remaining in
> the cabinet. This will be followed by others and a gen-
> eral shuffle, with the introduction of new men from both
> within and without parliament.
>
> *Toronto Telegram*, July 20, 1916

There was some fire behind that smoke, but when the cabinet
shuffle did come, it was not major and did not include
Cochrane. Perhaps the situation shouldn't have been put as
strongly as *Toronto Saturday Night* expressed it later: "Frank
Cochrane sick is worth a bag full of Reids, Burrells, Dohertys,
Meighens and Blondins in the pink of health." But there was
evidence then and later that Borden wanted Cochrane with
him as long as he would stay, even when they differed, as they
later did over the Union government of 1917.

For his part, Cochrane apparently had decided that as long
as he could be of use in the war cabinet, he would stay. His
experience was called upon extensively during 1915 and later
in one flaming issue of the war—the nickel question. It didn't
fall naturally into his department, but no minister knew the
industry as well as he did. Reports from the United States

said that some Canadian nickel was finding its way into enemy hands. The public was bombarding the government with protests that Canadian nickel was being used to kill Canadian soldiers overseas. A German submarine, the *Deutschland*, sailed from Baltimore with a cargo of nickel picked up from various U.S. refineries—which handled mainly Canadian ore. Although this cargo had been gathered from sources beyond Canadian government control, the heat was on.

Cochrane's involvement with nickel went back to his Sudbury days, when as mayor he had made the cause of the town's leading industry his own. In the 1890s Ontario had tried to arrange a British-controlled development of nickel resources in Canada, in which Ontario was willing to share the financing. The Admiralty turned it down, but in 1904 Britain asked that all future grants of nickel property should contain conditions guarding against foreign control. Cochrane, as Ontario mines minister in 1905, replied that practically all known nickel lands already had been granted or leased without such conditions. Nothing further was done until war broke out. Then the Ontario and the federal governments got together to safeguard future exports.

The principles laid down were agreed to by the British government, and on August 20, 1914, they were taken by Cochrane to the heads of the major nickel companies. The meeting was called in Ottawa by Cochrane. Included were Charles McCrea, Cochrane's successor as Ontario member for Sudbury and soon to become Ontario mines minister; Arthur Miles, president of Canadian Copper Company; and Ambrose Monell, president of Canadian Copper's U.S. parent, International Nickel Company. The main provision was for Canadian inspection and control of the refining of all nickel ore and matte shipments from Canada. An official of Cochrane's department, Graham Bell, made monthly trips to INCO headquarters in New York to prepare audited accounts of all nickel transactions—and for the sake of speed, was directed to report directly to Borden, who communicated the information in code to Britain.

This was all done unofficially, because a U.S. law forbade the passing of such information to a foreign power. But it worked so well that when there was a Canadian outcry urging a ban on all nickel shipments out of Canada, British Prime Minister Bonar Law issued a statement. He assured the Canadian public that the British government was satisfied with the arrangement and that an export ban would be disastrous to the supply lines for this metal.

The pressure to have the metal refined in Canada, however, was one area in which the government could act—for political reasons, if nothing else. Cochrane wrote a summary of the nickel situation to Borden, including these words: "I am just as anxious as anyone to see Canadian nickel refined in Canada, and I have advised the present companies that once it was shown that nickel could be refined on a commercial scale in Canada I would use my utmost endeavours to have the refining done in this country. . . ." On December 29, 1915, Cochrane drafted a letter to Monell, the head of INCO, and George Yates passed the draft to Borden. The letter urged Monell to set up in Canada "a nickel refinery . . . sufficient at least to supply the Canadian and Imperial requirements in case of trouble." Borden changed that last phrase to "under any conditions and in any emergency", asked for careful consideration, and signed the letter.

This resulted in INCO's making surveys which by the following summer led to a decision to build a nickel refinery at Port Colborne on Lake Erie. Bonar Law's initial reaction was an obvious indication of European war mentality, in which a border was too often a battleground. In a cable to the Canadian Governor General he said, "Army Council in view of military importance of proposed plants think question of site should be examined from point of view of security against possible invasion or hostile raids and that no site in the Niagara peninsula appears to fulfil above requirements." But somebody soon must have reminded Bonar Law about the undefended border and the safe friendship it reflected. He quickly withdrew his objection.

Cochrane during all this time was in precarious health, his kidney disease aggravated by the pressures of work, but once again the rumours of his retirement that were published in 1916 turned out to be premature. Cabinet changes did come in November that year, precipitated by the fact that General Sir Sam Hughes finally had become too much to be borne. Wrote Borden: "He was defiant of the government as well as of public opinion not only in the House of Commons but throughout the entire country." Especially he was embarrassing Canada every time he went abroad—and he went often. Now angry with Borden, he formed a plan to overthrow the government and confided this to a man who promptly told Borden. Borden appointed Sir George Perley as Minister of Overseas Forces, a new position, and Sir Edward Kemp to Hughes' Militia portfolio. Hughes remains to this day a controversial figure for his eccentricities as well as his achievements.

The 1917 session of Parliament, which followed two months later, has a special place in Canadian history. It started out softly enough, adjourning after a few weeks to allow Borden to attend the Imperial War Conference in London. When he left Canada in February, with about 435,000 Canadians in uniform and casualties to date of nearly 70,000, he felt that the voluntary system of enlistment had to be tried a while longer. He returned—after conferences with Canadian Army people overseas on the urgent problems of reinforcements—convinced that compulsory military service, conscription, was essential. He told the House immediately what he had in mind, realizing that he was risking a split in the country, Quebec versus the rest, but feeling that denial of adequate reinforcements would be a betrayal of the fighting men. Most of the country supported him. But some—including Laurier—could not.

From the beginning of the conscription debate, party lines began to crumble—there were conscriptionist Liberals, and anti-conscriptionist Conservatives. Borden felt that the way the Opposition was fighting looked like the work-up to forcing a general election on the issue.

Laurier had assented in 1916 to a one-year extension of the government's term. When Borden sounded him out on another extension, he got nowhere. Borden felt now that he had only two alternatives. In either case, he was determined to have conscription.

One alternative would be to fight a normal party-lines election and win that way if he could. The second would be to form a national coalition government made up of both Liberals and Conservatives, a united Win-the-War party. He asked Laurier to join him in forming such a government, and become part of it. If Laurier would do so, Borden offered to let him not only choose the Liberals in cabinet, but reject any Conservative he didn't like! Borden proposed that after this government was formed the conscription bill would be passed —but not enforced until after a general election.

Laurier refused in a letter dated June 6. A few days later Borden presented his Military Service Act to the Commons. From then on he worked actively at the Herculean task he had set for himself: to form a representative coalition despite Laurier's active opposition (which meant strong reluctance by many Liberals to join). On June 12 Borden sought and received the resignations of all his ministers. He felt he needed this freedom from commitments if he were to have any chance at all to form a coalition.

"A large majority of my colleagues were warm in their approval of my proposed course, a few were hesitant, and one, probably two, were distinctly hostile." On what evidence exists, Cochrane was among the hesitant or hostile. His son Wilbur said in 1970, "My father broke with Borden over the Union government idea." Certainly his resignation was terse enough: "Dear Sir Robert: I understand it is your desire to re-organize the government at this time. I beg, therefore, to place my resignation in your hands to do as you think best."

Even while approaching conscriptionist Liberals who might join him, Borden still abhorred the idea of a wartime election. So he tried once more to get by without it; to appeal to the whole House for an extension to October 7, 1918. He told his cabinet and caucus that unless assent was unanimous or nearly so he would not accept it. He also made this known to the House. Cochrane was among cabinet and private members who disputed Borden's insistence on near-unanimity. They felt that if the motion received any majority in the House, the extension should be accepted. Telegrams and letters from across the country said the same. Borden's motion for extension was carried by a majority of only twenty. Not enough. The next day, July 18, 1917, Borden announced that he was dropping the idea.

Now he was truly embarked on what Clifford Sifton already had defined as "the greatest political event ever accomplished in Canada"—*if* it could be done. That is, a coalition government. Borden's memoirs tell the story of that remarkable summer and autumn in detail: interminable conferences, placating his own people, courting and being courted by Liberals, receiving assurances from high Liberals that they would join a coalition if he would resign, the refusal of Conservatives to let him resign. Cochrane was already looking ahead to the election, telling Borden (August 12), "we cannot win unless we win at least half the constituencies in the west." It was near midnight on October 11 when the final few pieces fell into place, and Borden had his Union cabinet, with nine Liberals, one token labour representative, and thirteen Conservatives. Cochrane had given up Railways and Canals to his old stand-in, J. D. Reid, but remained as a minister without portfolio with the promise—although this was not to be—that he would become chairman of Canadian Northern Railways when taken over by the government, and later chief executive of an amalgamation of all government railways.

There seems little doubt that his decision to stay in the government, organize Ontario for the Win-the-War election, and run as a Union candidate himself in Temiskaming (against Arthur E. Roebuck) was predicated on wanting to finish the job; not only the job of bringing business-like order to government railways in Canada, which had been so chaotic when he began, but also to do what he could to see the war brought to a successful conclusion.

Already, he could see the probability of certain things that would be left undone. No more funds were to be spent on the Hudson Bay Railway, at least until after the war, and he must have doubted he would be around to see the resumption. The Intercolonial was a counterbalance, doing so well under his reorganization man, Gutelius, that its profits were the highest they'd ever been. But from time to time there had been what George Yates called "great and bitter disappointments". One of these had come on September 11, 1916, when Cochrane conducted a high government party to Quebec to watch an historic event: the hoisting into place of the 600-foot central span of the Quebec bridge. Cochrane, his party, and the principal engineers visited the main portion of the bridge that morning before breakfast and were elated at the prospects that soon trains would be running over it, completing the National Transcontinental's eastern division, begun twelve years before. They left the bridge and returned to their ship, the *Lady Grey*, anchored a couple of hundred yards downstream. A huge crowd lined both banks of the river. The suspended span was manoeuvred into position, hoisting links were attached, and the span was raised thirty feet off the water before work was temporarily stopped for breakfast. Cochrane and his party were watching with the others a little later when work resumed and the hoists again took the strain. First a casting split, dropping the southwest corner of the span. Then the centre began to buckle and twist; like molasses, one observer said. As watchers shouted in shock, Yates later wrote, "With a tremendous crash it twisted and toppled into the river." Ten lives were lost, and (Yates again): "The loss of so much valuable steel in wartime was in itself a great tragedy, almost a calamity."

He'd been living with the steel problem, along with Cochrane, and he knew.

The collapse was crushing enough that after a quick investigation, Cochrane decided that his department would not waste time with recriminations or penalty claims; the important thing was still to get the bridge built. The builders, instead of being taken to court, were offered incentives by Cochrane for an early completion. On the next time, September 20, 1917, all went well. Trains were running over the bridge by late October. The delay had been just over one year.

Cochrane's commitment to the war effort may have been no more than that of most men in similar positions but some of his strong attitudes showed in one debate in mid 1917. Steel was so hard to find by then that Cochrane, even with all new railway construction halted, still had to lift rails from completed sections of the National Transcontinental to ship to France for use by Canadian railroad-building battalions there. Just any second-hand rails would not do; they had to be of a certain type. Since there was no available surplus of that type, lines already laid had to be cannibalized. Details had been given to Laurier in January, but in May and again in July Cochrane was under fire in Commons for his choice of where these rails were being removed. Frank Oliver of Edmonton led the attack, because some of the rails were coming from his constituency. In this debate Cochrane showed a fire rare to him, indicating strongly the depth of his passionate feelings about doing what he was asked to help the war effort. Oliver was claiming that the rails should be bought elsewhere and Bennett had just interjected that they would cost $100 a ton or more, and weren't to be found anywhere anyway.

> Oliver: I saw in yesterday's papers that the Russian Government is able to make a contract with firms in the United States for supplying locomotives. Could not they make a contract for an equal value of steel rails if they had paid the price? I think they could. My hon. friend

mentioned $100 a ton. I ask you, Sir, will $100 a ton pay the damages to the Grand Trunk Railway Company, to my constituents, and to the people of Canada resulting from the tearing up of these tracks? I say it will not begin to pay it, and an honest endeavour to do the best that could be done to help the war in France would have caused this Government to secure those rails from the United States at whatever price was necessary rather than tear up the rails in our own country, thereby discommoding our own people, discrediting our own enterprise, and in the end charging the British Government two or three times as much as they should have paid.

. . . I am a supporter of the Hudson Bay railway; I believe that that road should be pushed to completion, and pushed to completion at the earliest day. But if the Government is not going to use these rails for the Hudson Bay road, and is not going to finish the road, then why not use these rails instead of tearing up the rails of the Grand Trunk Pacific west of Edmonton?

Cochrane: I am more than surprised at the extravagant statements made by the hon. member for Edmonton [Mr. Oliver]. He seems to know more about what rails are required and what rails should go forward for use at the front than the British Government do. These rails are laid under fire in many cases, and the British Government have asked us to send rails of the same borings and the same kind as before, so that they may be laid as easily and as quickly as possible. And now the statement is made again that we are bound to ruin the construction of the Grand Trunk Pacific and Transcontinental. It is all bosh—nothing but bosh. I have heard a great deal from the other side of the House to the effect that we have degraded the line and all that kind of thing. Why, that is all wrong; it is impossible. It is as good a road as ever has been laid; it has never been degraded in any sense of the word. I defy any one to prove it.

Oliver: Then why tear it up?

Cochrane: I would tear up the whole Transcontinental, yes, and every other railway in Canada, to win this war.

Oliver: But you don't ask something from the Canadian Pacific Railway?

Cochrane: Because, I tell you, the Canadian Pacific Railway rails have different borings. (Aside) I would like to send him to the front, by Heavens, to lay these rails.

Oliver: I want him to understand that I am represented at the front. Is he?

Cochrane: I know you are, but you don't talk as if you were. The hon. gentleman's talk is for pure politics, and nothing else. He thinks his chances for re-election are so bad that he will have to make use of everything, turning this whole war into a political game, instead of fighting it out as he ought.

Turriff: That is what the Government has done from the start.

Cochrane: No, they have not.

Pugsley: This minister says that he is going to tear up all the rails in Canada in order to win the war.

Cochrane: No, I did not say that.

Pugsley: If necessary to win the war. That is a very laudable desire and I think we would all agree to it if it were necessary to win the war. . . . There is another serious phase to this question. The interruption at this time of the operation of a great coal mine in western Canada is a matter of the most serious character.

Cochrane: Will the interruption of the operation of that coal mine or the interruption of the prosecution of the war at the front be the more serious matter for Canada?

Pugsley: I should like to see both carried on. I should like to see no interruption of the collieries operation, and no interruption of the war.

Cochrane: You do not speak like it.

George Yates noted in 1950 that Cochrane was "obliged to take extended rest on doctor's orders" during 1917, but, as in the matter of rails for the front, most debates touching railroad matters found him in his place. On June 11, 1917, he delivered what was to be his final annual statement on the work of his department. From it, one gets an idea of the scope

his domain now had: 4,063 miles of railroad, all of it east
of Winnipeg; difficulties in obtaining coal supplies due to the
war; nearly six million passengers carried without a fatal
accident . . .

> Pugsley: The minister speaks of there being no loss of
> life. My information is that in one week last winter
> there were 20 train wrecks; 20 locomotives being
> thrown off the track. Does the minister make any refer-
> ence to that?
> Cochrane: I do not.
> Pugsley: The minister only makes reference to loss of
> life, not to train wrecks.
> Cochrane: The hon. member would like to gain a
> political point; that is his idea.

Cochrane's account went on: . . . troop trains so well
handled that no ship had ever to wait at Halifax for its load of
fighting men, although trains sometimes had to wait for ships.
The Halifax Terminals had been enlarged; grain elevators
built at Transcona, Manitoba; passenger cars re-fitted to act as
hospital cars. Car repairmen worked so hard that the list of
damaged and out-of-duty freight cars had been reduced from
1410 to 400 during the year. Work on the Hudson Bay Railway was slowing to a stop; work had been suspended on the
Welland Ship Canal until war's end; the Trent Canal work
was almost complete. It was a long catalogue of what had been
his main concern for five years, a work now almost over,
for him.

That autumn, without a department in his charge any
longer, he was as active in the election campaign as his health
would permit. Mostly he was organizing, directing. He still
had the power. There was a mixup in Algoma East. W. R.
Smyth, by then a lieutenant-colonel in England, was asked to
run—but Cochrane already had decided upon G. B. Nicholson
as the candidate, and was urging a Senate seat for Smyth.
Cochrane cabled Smyth: "Rumoured you have cabled accepting Union nomination. Nicholson in field. Rest assured we will
look after you. Wire Robb definite withdrawal. F. Cochrane."

The withdrawal was cabled immediately. It was a tough, man-scarring national campaign, including posters which read: A Vote for Laurier is a Vote for the Kaiser. Win-the-War committees sprang up all over, and Borden's Union Government candidates often advertised themselves by that slogan: Win-the-War. Cochrane won his own seat easily in Temiskaming, although it included many French-Canadian anti-conscriptionists. Across the country the big vote was for Union Government and its main reason-for-being, conscription: 153 seats out of a total of 235. Laurier's 82 included only 20 seats outside of Quebec; 10 of these were in the Maritimes and 8 in eastern Ontario. From mid Ontario to the Pacific Ocean, only two Laurier candidates were elected.

A few days after the election Cochrane travelled to New York to undergo treatment by a specialist he had been visiting in secret (according to Yates) for several years, a doctor originally recommended by Sir William Mackenzie. His regular work in government was almost over. In 1918 he relieved Burrell temporarily as Secretary of State, and Reid in Railways and Canals. Yates, no longer with enough to occupy him in Cochrane's office, became Borden's private secretary. Cochrane attended cabinet regularly through the brightening last months of the war, but at the same time found himself again at the centre of a national controversy. Parliament had decided in 1917 to acquire the balance of capital stock in the Canadian Northern. A Board of Arbitration held hearings to determine the value. The press followed the hearings with great interest and sensational exploiting of some evidence. Once the decision had been made to pay Mackenzie and Mann $8,500,000 for their shares, the next item of business was: who will run it?

Cochrane felt he had been promised the job. There is little doubt he was right. In Borden's papers appears (marked: Memo, 1917) a draft announcement of Cochrane's appointment to the job he never got. It lauds Cochrane's record as grounds for the choice, referring to his improved health, and is edited in Borden's handwriting. But that draft never was re-typed, the announcement never made.

By September of 1918, the public knew that a chairman and board of directors soon would be named not only for the Canadian Northern, but also for a new grouping of the government-owned National Transcontinental, Intercolonial, and lesser lines, a mileage of 13,700. The *Sunday World* reported, "The Hon. Frank Cochrane is still confident that he will get the coveted position. . . . Gossip says there is deadlock in the cabinet, and a friend said this morning, 'Cochrane is a proud man and he feels he is being treated like a child.' " (The friend might have been R. B. Bennett, mentioned elsewhere at the time as being on Cochrane's side.) "But Frank Cochrane views things philosophically. He refers humorously to solicitude about his health manifested by people not heretofore friendly. He quietly takes it for granted that whatever pledge was made to him . . . will be kept."

The *Globe* attacked Cochrane hotly, all the way back to his bringing in Bourassa in the 1911 election as a means of "fanning religious hatred", and said: "His administration was marked by many arbitrary acts and by frequent absences because of ill health." The *News* remade its editorial page that day, September 14, to answer the *Globe*: "The arbitrary acts referred to were doubtless those by which Mr. Cochrane eliminated patronage and political wire pulling in the management of the Intercolonial Railway. His course was a complete reversal of the corrupt methods long pursued by the Globe's friends in the management of that transportation system." This was the reason, said the *News*, for the *Globe*'s "vindictive pursuit of a man who did more to purify the administration of the national railways than all his predecessors put together."

Meanwhile, Borden was trying to make his peace with the many who wrote to him supporting Cochrane for this natural final goal in his career. One was James E. Day, Toronto lawyer and mining man. To Day, Borden lauded Cochrane on all counts except one: "The difficulty in his case is his physical condition. .... I am exceedingly apprehensive that any resumption of duties so exacting as those which have been suggested would within a few weeks or months break down his health permanently. His physician in New York is of this opinion and I believe this view is shared by his physician in Toronto."

A few days later Borden appointed D. B. Hanna as chairman of Canadian Northern. On November 18, an order-in-council made Hanna chairman of all government railways—soon to be known as the Canadian National Railways. Time and illness had overtaken Cochrane, finally.

That year, 1918, Cochrane's son Ogden was injured in a training accident in England. Invalided home, he spent many months in hospital, and died in January 1919. "This was a sad blow to his people and particularly severe on his father, whose own health by this time had become precarious," Yates wrote. Still, Cochrane testified a little later before the commission investigating the navigability of Hudson Bay and Hudson Straits.

"At one time I was Minister of Railways and Canals in the Canadian government," he began. It was a wistful moment for those listening who remembered him in his full power, only two years earlier. That appearance was almost his last act as a Canadian politician.

On September 22, 1919, away from Ottawa because he, too, was ill, Borden wrote in his diary: "Cochrane died this morning at 3:30. I sent a letter of condolence to Mrs. Cochrane. Also sent my appreciation [of him] to the press. He was an outstanding figure, a man of very strong character, always a true and loyal friend. For some years illness had left its trace on his great ability."

Cochrane died in the family apartment in Ottawa's Roxborough. That afternoon, with Borden away, C. J. Doherty rose as acting prime minister to pay the official tribute of the House.

"We and the people of Canada have known him as a man who throughout a lengthy career earned a reputation for sterling integrity, and whose every action was inspired by a desire to do his duty, and to do it in full measure," he said. "Not only in his private life was he distinguished by those qualities, but he brought them to the service of the people, first of his own province and then of this Dominion. I am satisfied that this House would desire to pay to him that tribute of respect and admiration which his devotion to the public service, the sterling qualities that he brought to that service, and the splendid record that he leaves behind him, command."

The following day Doherty moved an early adjournment in the House to allow members to follow Cochrane's remains from his home to the railway station bound for the funeral to be held in Toronto. When the members returned to the House late in the day, Doherty rose again. He noted that because the funeral the next day was not taking place in Ottawa, many members could not attend "and pay that last tribute of respect to our departed friend". But he moved that when the House adjourned that evening, it remain adjourned until four on the following afternoon. "In this way we shall refrain from carrying on the business of the House for the period of time during which the funeral ceremony will take place."

Cochrane was buried in Mount Pleasant Cemetery on September 24, 1919, alongside his son Ogden. His widow lived another twenty years in Ottawa before her death.

He is rarely spoken of now, Canada being a country where few politicians below the rank of prime minister are accorded a ready place in history. But he had a discernible influence on his time and the future of his country. His own frontier background and gruff love and understanding of the mines and forests, and of northerners, was translated into Ontario legislation that set a sometimes innovative standard for other provinces. The major canal systems of today are based on his impetus of more than a half-century ago. Under his hand (and under a principle he once tossed off in a Commons debate: "I don't see why a railway, just because it is government-owned should not be run on a businesslike basis"), government ownership of railways made long strides toward an efficiency and respectability which had eluded it until Cochrane came along.

But he was a plain man. As the *Canadian Annual Review* once noted, covering his activities for 1912, he spoke rarely during the year under review "but did a lot of interesting things". So he did not leave behind the phrases of eloquence that help to make men better remembered and by which—if Cochrane had left them—one could better sum up his life. Others did try. Borden, being a plain man himself, wrote about Cochrane in 1927 (to R. B. Bennett): "Throughout my political career I never met a minister more wholly swayed by considerations of public interest and less influenced by party consideration than Frank Cochrane." Add Whitney's handwritten, "There is no stronger man in the province than Mr. Cochrane." And R. B. Bennett's "He is the really strong man in the government. . . . A great silent man with a vision of the future of Canada which he cannot express." Then see him with his long thin face and figure, sitting on the stage of a smoky Northern Ontario Opera House while George Gordon, or Charles LaMarche, or some other northern spellbinder pours on the flowery introduction, and Cochrane rises and starts giving it to the audience straight and without embellishment, and you have the picture of the man and his time.

A NOTE ON SOURCES

A researcher worked for eight months in the Public Archives of Canada, investigating and recording every mention of Frank Cochrane in the House of Commons debates and proceedings, 1911 to 1919. The authors found much useful material in the papers of Sir Robert Borden, Sir Thomas White, and others. In the Ontario Archives the papers of Sir James Pliny Whitney were especially useful. The Ontario Legislative Library helped greatly with clippings of newspaper reports on legislative sittings before shorthand records of debates were kept. A complete microfilm record of the old *Sudbury Journal* from 1891 to 1918 was read and portions noted. Articles, editorials, and feature stories in many other newspapers of the time were checked.

We are indebted to Mr. William I. Hearst, of Toronto, for providing us with first-hand recollections as well as anecdotes passed on by his father, Sir William Hearst. A few letters and clippings—very few—had been kept by Frank Cochrane's descendants.

Cochrane's son Wilbur gave us an interview in 1970 when he was eighty-six years of age. (He died a year later.) As a youth Wilbur often travelled with his father. His quick and fragmentary recollections filled in some gaps.

Several photo albums and scrapbooks had been kept by Cochrane's private secretary, George W. Yates. His photos of an inspection trip Cochrane made of the route of the Hudson Bay Railway in 1912 were especially complete.

INDEX